A N O T H E R

O N E
A R
N E
O H
T

*The New Testament
Prescription for Transformation*

DAVID A. deSILVA

Seedbed

Printed in the United States of America

Cover design by Strange Last Name
Page design by and layout by PerfecType, Nashville, Tennessee

DeSilva, David Arthur.
   One another : the New Testament prescription for transformation / David A. DeSilva. – Franklin, Tennessee : Seedbed Publishing, ©2021.

       pages ; cm .

       ISBN 9781628249125 (paperback)
       ISBN 9781628249163 (DVD)
       ISBN 9781628249132 (Mobi)
       ISBN 9781628249149 (ePub)
       ISBN 9781628249156 (uPDF)
       OCLC 1266859752

       1. Fellowship–Biblical teaching. 2. Christian life–Methodist authors.
       3. Bible. New Testament—Criticism, interpretation, etc. I. Title.

BS2545.F4 D37 2021   248.4/861   2021946486

SEEDBED PUBLISHING
Franklin, Tennessee
seedbed.com

To Stephen A. Naughton

"Do not abandon old friends,
for new ones cannot equal them." (Sir. 9:10)

Contents

Introduction

"I can be a Christian without going to church."

"I believe in Jesus, but the church really turns me off."

"My faith is something between me and my God."

The chances are good that many of us have heard these or similar statements from people when the conversation turns to church or, perhaps, when we have reached out to invite someone to come experience worship and other facets of the life of our churches. Some of us may even have uttered statements like these at some point in our lives.

The truth is, while we ourselves might go to church and even like the people at church, many of us might still think that how we live the Christian life really is something between us and God (or between us and Christ). While we will go to church, we may go with our personal boundaries raised fairly high, enjoying friendly interactions while keeping one another at arm's length—and keeping our faith or our life choices safe from other Christians poking their noses too close into our business. We're glad to interact pleasantly on the way into and out from worship, in and around the refreshments, and at potluck dinners. We might even be glad to interact pleasantly for an additional hour in a Sunday school or Bible study group. But, in general, we really may not want the conversations to get too close to home and we exercise all sorts of diversionary tactics if we feel something is getting too personal. We may be reluctant to share the struggles that we're facing in our faith journey or just in our lives and relationships, because we don't want to be judged on any basis beyond the façade we project to manage impressions. And we may be so involved in our own lives and schedules, in which we have left so little room for others, that we become profoundly uncomfortable when someone presents a genuine need and asks for help.

To the extent that we might see ourselves or other members of our congregation reflected in this picture, we are collectively missing out (and causing others to miss out) on one of the greatest and most important resources that Christ has given us to help us in our journey through life and through a life of faithful discipleship—*one another*. We are missing out on the gifts that other believers can be (and are meant to be) to us and we are likely withholding from them the gifts that Christ intends for us to be to them.

The writings in the New Testament have a great deal to say about the quality of the relationships, the level of the interactions, and the depth of the interventions Christians are to cultivate among and to offer one another. The New Testament does not cast a vision for merely polite and friendly casual interactions. Rather, it casts a vision for significant investment in one another's lives; for bestowing significant value on one another that we will not take back with the first disagreement or conflict; for giving one another permission to be who they are in Christ; for allowing one another room to try and to fail and to disappoint; and room to speak the truth to us in love when we try and fail and disappoint, knowing that we will still be in loving relationship with one another on the other side of temporary turmoil.

There is a moment in many services of baptism when the pastor addresses the congregation with the question: "Will you nurture one another in the Christian faith and life and include these persons now before you in your care?" The response that the members of these congregations make, speaking in unison, is striking:

> With God's help we will proclaim the good news
> and live according to the example of Christ. We will

surround *these persons* with a community of love and forgiveness, that *they* may grow in *their* trust of God, and be found faithful in *their* service to others. We will pray for *them*, that *they* may be true disciples who walk in the way that leads to life.[1]

This is a promise that everyone present at every baptismal service has made in the churches I have served since 1995. We promise, in regard to everyone who comes forward for baptism, that we will keep reminding those new Christians in word and example of the good news of Jesus and the new life that the good news is meant to awaken and empower. We promise to invest ourselves in loving those new Christians and offering our forgiveness as they work to leave behind the practices of their old person and grow more comfortable (even as we continue to grow) in the practices of the new person that the Spirit is bringing to life. We promise to be the sort of friends—indeed, the sort of family—for them that will move them to trust God more and will help keep them steady in their own investment of themselves in the lives of others. We promise to hold their continued progress toward holiness before God in prayer, invoking God's

1. "The Baptismal Covenant I" *United Methodist Hymnal*, 40, italics in original. See https://www.umcdiscipleship.org/resources/the-baptismal-covenant-i.

favor and help (and listening for ways in which God would position us to *be* the help that he would offer). In this magnificent pledge, we take on specific duties and responsibilities toward one another—and ought, therefore, to be able to rely upon one another to provide.

This pledge begins to reflect the kind of community that the New Testament writers so passionately wanted Christ's followers to be for one another. Those early Christian leaders who planted and tended the assemblies of converts in Corinth, Galatia, Ephesus, Philippi, and the like recognized that the steady progress of any individual disciple as he or she moves out from being driven by the flesh toward being fully Spirit-led required the investment, intervention, and support of other disciples. This was a conviction shared by John Wesley. Indeed, it proved foundational to the method and the structure by means of which he sought to bring renewal to the Church of England, and that remained foundational to the movement after it emerged as an independent denomination. Wesley's method was to band disciples together in small circles that would meet regularly to inquire into one another's spiritual successes and struggles, encouraging one another, holding one another accountable, and praying for one another's perseverance in their journey toward ever fuller holiness of heart and life.

The experience of the love of God and the joy of the Holy Spirit went hand in hand with the experience of authentic community from the earliest days of the church's existence. The hunger for authentic community has not diminished in the almost two intervening millennia, and the New Testament writings—the church's charter documents— urge us to invest ourselves in creating and sustaining this experience for one another. In this study, we will look together—and hopefully discuss quite honestly together— the New Testament vision for our relationships, interactions, and interventions with one another in a local Christian community. This vision impels us to encourage and support one another, offering reinforcement for holy living that, according to the apostles, we owe one another as the people not only welcomed into relationship with God through Jesus Christ, but given as gifts to one another for this very purpose.

As Paul urged the Christians in Rome, so he continues to urge us: "let's strive for the things that bring peace and the things that build each other up" (Rom. 14:19 CEB).

Using This Book in an Adult Bible Study or Small Group

While this book can be read profitably by an individual, it is more ideally suited (as one might expect from a book entitled *One Another*) to being explored together with other Christians. It can be used in any group setting from the morning Sunday school class to the midweek Bible study to the evening home group. The successful use of this book in such a setting, however, depends upon the participants' committed engagement during the week in between group sessions. Ideally, participants will keep journals of some sort to record their reflections on the questions that punctuate each chapter so that they can share with greater detail during the weekly group meeting.

Readers will notice that each chapter contains questions not only for reflection and discussion, but also for action. As with all effective Bible studies, this resource seeks to push readers to discover the ways in which God would shape their practice through engagement with the Word. Each week's meeting should give time not only to what participants have learned or thought, but also to what they have done or plan concretely to do as a result of their prayerful study.

A simple plan for each group session might take the following form:

1. Open with prayer.
2. View accompanying video.
3. Identify key ideas from the first section of the chapter assigned for the week.
4. Discuss responses to the questions for reflection, discussion, and action that close that section.

5. Repeat #3 and #4 for each succeeding section of the week's chapter.
6. Review action steps to be taken in the coming week.
7. Close with prayer.

You may, of course, pray in your own way using your own words; however, if you wish, you may also use the opening and closing prayers provided.

1

Who Are We to
One Another?

Opening Prayer for Session One

Give us open ears, O Lord, to hear you speaking to us through your Holy Scriptures and through your holy people, our sisters and brothers. Let us clearly discern what your Holy Spirit would say to us this day and let us be sure to obey so that, in our lives and in our life together, we may ever more fully reflect your good and holy desires for us. We ask this in the name of Jesus, our Lord and Redeemer. Amen.

How would you describe your relationship with those other people who show up with you at 9:30 a.m. on

Sunday mornings? Is your relationship like that of members of an audience who converge at a theater for the same matinee, take in the performance, and go your separate ways (perhaps after sharing some words of appreciation for—or criticism of—the lead players with one another over refreshments)? Fortunately, I have not personally encountered many people who feel *quite* so unattached to their fellow believers who assemble for morning worship.

Perhaps the model of the voluntary association or organization—like the Kiwanis or Rotary—better describes how a good number of Christians would categorize their relationships with one another. Voluntary associations were known in various forms in the first century and in various forms today. During the first century, people might join a guild related to their trade as a means of social networking and, occasionally, mutual assistance, or they might join a more overtly religious club and be initiated into the mysteries of Dionysus, Isis, or some other deity. We join with others in a voluntary association on the basis of a common interest or affinity and we associate with them in cordial ways as long as it suits us, or as long as it is in our mutual interest to do so, or as long as we are not too greatly put out or put off by one or more members of that particular group. But we can drop in and drop out of such groups, and we really have no expectation of long-term commitment to the group or to one another beyond what our individual inclinations and inertia afford.

The degree to which your congregation experiences the phenomenon of church-hopping might be taken as an indicator of our general level of commitment to the particular people around us in the local assembly. There are certainly circumstances under which it is right and good to break one's ties with a given congregation in favor of joining a new congregation, generally when one truly believes that the first church is moving in a direction that would violate one's conscience or understanding of God's call on the lives of those God has redeemed. But those circumstances seem to account for only a fraction of the movement between congregations that I myself have witnessed. More often, it seems, church-hopping is one more manifestation of our fight-or-flight instinct: we get into a fight with someone at our local congregation (often someone in some leadership capacity) and we take flight to another church or, in a worst-case scenario, to no church.

Wherever this happens, the phenomenon suggests that our relationships are not very deep, so there is not a high emotional cost to leaving. Unfortunately, we do not foster a church culture that expects people to stay and work through any issues despite knowing that it is precisely in such work that the Spirit transforms us and our relationships for the better.

The images for the church that we encounter throughout the New Testament challenge us to examine ourselves for any hint of an "I can take them or leave them" attitude concerning our brothers and sisters in Christ. They challenge any notion that we are connected and bound only by shared interests—and only so long as no conflicts arise. Rather, they drive us toward accepting a significant and shared responsibility to and for one another—a responsibility laid upon us by the God who called us together in Christ. While this responsibility ultimately is laid upon all members of the global church, it is fired and refined most fully and consistently in the local assemblies—and in smaller, intentional groups within the local assemblies—which provide the fundamental context for living life together in Christ.

• Questions for Reflection and Discussion •

To what extent do you think of your faith (and that of other Christians) as a private matter between you and God?

What is your level of attachment, involvement, and commitment to the people in your local congregation?

• • •

The images used by New Testament writers to speak of the church, both in its global totality and in any given local manifestation, are all *collective* images. They are images in which the individual member's significance is found in his or her place as a vital part of the larger whole.

The image that most pervades the New Testament is the image of family. Indeed, to speak of this as an "image" is to speak too timidly about the assertions made throughout the early Christian Scriptures. Being family is the new reality for those who have attached themselves to Jesus. Jesus himself is remembered to have begun this process of redefining family. On one occasion, as he was teaching a large group in something like a house, his mother and his brothers were standing outside and seeking to get in a word with him. When someone told Jesus about them, he replied:

> "Who is my mother, and who are my brothers?" Pointing to his disciples, he said, "Here are my mother and my brothers! For whoever does the will of my Father in heaven is my brother and sister and mother." (Matt. 12:48b–50 NIV; see also Mark 3:33–35; Luke 8:21)

While this word would no doubt have been difficult for his biological family to hear and process, it clearly articulated Jesus' vision for the kind of community his followers would offer to one another. They were to share with one another the level of attention, commitment, and investment that was normally reserved for one's blood relations. Jesus spoke this in an environment in which following him would typically provoke rejection by one's blood relations. Those who suffered being ostracized and cut off from their natural families for Jesus' sake would be able to find a new and larger family among Jesus' followers. Because of the emotional, social, and often material support of this new family, the many alienated individual followers of Jesus would be able to persevere in their commitment to him and not succumb to the social pressures seeking to shame them into turning back from that commitment.

As Jesus assured Peter and all who followed him:

> "There is no one who has left house or brothers or sisters or mother or father or children or fields, for my sake and for the sake of the good news, who will not receive a hundredfold now in this age—houses, brothers and sisters, mothers and children, and fields, with persecutions—and in the age to come eternal life." (Mark 10:29–30)

Finding in one's fellow followers of Jesus a family that would take the place of the natural relatives that they left behind—or that dissociated themselves from the Christ-follower—remains critically important for believers in hostile environments around the world today. But it is also a critically important network of encouragement, support, and companionship if disciples in *any* environment are to attain the heights of the holiness and commitment to which Christ calls us all.

Early Christian preachers latched onto this facet of Jesus' teaching and pushed it even further. Paul, for example, spoke of Jesus' achievement on our behalf in terms of bringing about our adoption into God's family.

> In Christ Jesus you are all sons [and daughters] of God, through faith. (Gal. 3:26 ESV)

> But when the fullness of time had come, God sent forth his Son, born of a woman, born under the law, to redeem those who were under the law, so that we might receive adoption as sons [and daughters]. And because you are sons [and daughters], God has sent the Spirit of his Son into our hearts, crying, "Abba! Father!" (Gal. 4:4–6 ESV)

Jesus, Paul, and other New Testament voices call us to bestow upon one another the status of being our family as a necessary consequence of God's bestowing upon me, upon you, upon him, and upon her, the status of being God's sons and daughters together. The adoption of which Galatians 4:4–6 and other texts speak is an adoption into a new household, a new family, and not into a merely private relationship that *I* enjoy with God. And together with acknowledging one another as the family that God has brought together, the family that God has given to each one of us, we are called to show one another the care, commitment, and mutual responsibility that we owe one another as family. We might define family—somewhat tongue-in-cheek—as the people you can't really get rid of, the people who remain with you in some sense even when you're not together, not agreeing, perhaps not even speaking. This is even truer of the family that God has brought together, for he has done so for eternity. What would our relationships with other Christians look like if we gave these relationships the priority that such a faith claim makes on their behalf?

Far and away the most common term used to name or address another Christian in the early church is "brother" or "sister."[1] New Testament authors speak of the global Christian community as a "brotherhood and sisterhood" (1 Peter 2:17; 5:9) and on several occasions specifically lift up "brotherly and sisterly love" (in Greek, *philadelphia*) as

---

1. This is more evident in translations like the NASB or ESV that are not committed to using gender-inclusive language, though some that do strive for gender-inclusive language, like the NIV 2011, are also able to maintain the language of "brothers and sisters" more than others. The NRSV, for example, frequently renders the Greek words that ought to be translated as "brothers" or "brothers and sisters" as "believers," or the Greek word for "brotherly/sisterly love" as "mutual love," thus muting the element of kinship that was and remains so central to Christian identity and ethos.

the particular species of love that Christians are to show one another (Rom. 12:9–10; 1 Thess. 4:9–10; Heb. 13:1; 1 Peter 1:22; 3:8; 2 Peter 1:7). It is, of course, appropriate that the sibling relationship should emerge as the particular family relationship that we all share with one another, since we have all been adopted together by the same Parent into his family thanks to the mediation of the one "natural" Son in the divine household. Many facets of the ethos that the New Testament writers sought to nurture are related to this most basic identification of one another as "family" and, particularly, as "brothers and sisters." The relationship shared by siblings was generally held to be the closest and most enduring of relationships in the first-century context. And we will see as the study continues to unfold, that a great deal of how we are urged to treat one another in the New Testament reflects the ideal behavior of brothers and sisters toward each other in Greek and Roman ethical writings. Sharing resources with one another, prioritizing unity and seeking to live harmoniously with one another, cooperating rather than competing with one another, forgiving one another—these were all ways in which natural siblings were urged to behave in their interactions with one another.

• Questions for Reflection and Discussion •

Can you describe an occasion or a season in which you have experienced in Christian circles the close attachment, personal support, and strong commitment that made you feel like family one to another?

What reservations do you have about engaging (or what obstacles do you see needing to be overcome in order to engage) other Christian believers as family?

• • •

A second image for the church found throughout the second half of the New Testament is that of a building. This is a metaphor that overtook the reality as churches came to refer to physical buildings in which Christians gathered rather than identifying the gathered Christians as (part of) the spiritual building that God was fitting together for God's own dwelling. Such confusion was not yet possible in the first century or two of the Christian movement's existence, before Christians began building separate structures dedicated to the common life and worship of the local community of believers. Rather, they understood that the gathering of Christ-followers *was* the "church," as reflected, for example, in Paul's statement: "When you come together *as* a church" (1 Cor. 11:18, emphasis added), never "*in* a church." In such a context, the authors of 1 Peter and of Ephesians could liken the growth of the global community of Christ-followers to the construction of a new kind of temple for God's dwelling:

> Come to him, a living stone, though rejected by mortals yet chosen and precious in God's sight, and like living stones, let yourselves be built into a spiritual house, to be a holy priesthood, to offer spiritual sacrifices acceptable to God through Jesus Christ. (1 Peter 2:4–5)

> In [Christ] the whole structure is joined together and grows into a holy temple in the Lord; in whom you also are built together spiritually into a dwelling place for God. (Eph. 2:21–22)

A stone, no matter how well shaped and polished, is not much of a temple. But as such stones are brought together— so these authors would suggest—a suitable house for God comes into being. Sacred space has always been important to human beings in their quest for the divine; these New Testament authors make the bold claim that such sacred space is not architectural, but social. It is the space occupied by those who have been made new in Christ and, as those who have received mercy, have been made a new people together (1 Peter 2:10). We know God's presence and offer to God the worship and service that is God's due more fully when we come together collectively as the temple in which

God dwells and collectively as the "holy priesthood" that has been consecrated together as agents for divine service.

A third image is that of a body, a single entity composed of many distinct parts, a single whole no part of which can be cut off from another except in the direst circumstances and never without deep sorrow, pain, and awareness of loss. The image, prominent in the letters of Paul, was developed first by Greek philosophers reflecting on the cosmos as a whole. These philosophers likened the universe to a single, complex organism. It was a body of which all living beings and other facets of material creation were parts, contributing their various functions to the overall working of the whole, and within which God was the animating soul. Paul seized on the image to describe the Christian community, both local and global, animated by the Holy Spirit as its unifying and life-giving force.

> For as in one body we have many members, and not all the members have the same function, so we, who are many, are one body in Christ, and individually we are members one of another. (Rom. 12:4–5)

> For just as the body is one and has many members, and all the members of the body, though many, are one body, so it is with Christ. For in the one Spirit we were all baptized into one body—Jews or Greeks,

slaves or free—and we were all made to drink of one Spirit. Indeed, the body does not consist of one member but of many. . . . If the whole body were an eye, where would the hearing be? If the whole body were hearing, where would the sense of smell be? But as it is, God arranged the members in the body, each one of them, as he chose. . . . The eye cannot say to the hand, "I have no need of you," nor again the head to the feet, "I have no need of you.". . . Now you are the body of Christ and individually members of it. (1 Cor. 12:12–14, 17–18, 21, 27)

The image allows Paul to drive home several points about Christians in community. The focus of God's redemptive action is not on *me* living out *my* faith well, but on *us* living out *our* faith well in a coordinated fashion with one another. No one of us can accomplish all that needs to take place for Christian community to function properly and flourish. No one of us can achieve God's vision for us on our own, because God's vision is a vision for an *us* and not a *me*. Those who say that they can be Christian without "going to church" (that is, without "coming together as a church") and those who believe that their faith is a "private matter between me and God" have either rejected or not grasped Paul's gospel. Paul wanted Christ-followers to understand that each one of them was more akin to a hand or an eye or a liver—vital when embedded in and working as part of the whole, but something else entirely when disconnected from the whole. The image of a body made up of many parts drives home the fundamental interdependence that Christians share with one another and, by implication, the systemic dysfunction that results when we fail to fulfill our function on behalf of the whole body.

Brothers and sisters in one, great family. Stones fitted together into God's own dwelling. The many parts of a well-functioning and flourishing body. These images provide us with points of entry into how we are to think about our connection with one another—namely, that this connection is *central* to our Christian identity. They also guide us as we think about our responses to and responsibilities for one another. God has joined us together for eternity and joined us together now for our own and one another's eternal good.

God's Spirit indeed lives in each one of us, but there is another, indispensable dimension of encountering God as a result of our having been brought together with and joined to one another. God has placed each of us in the context of the larger body—whether we conceive of this in terms of our local Christian assembly or in terms of the global body of Christ—so that we could receive the benefits of what other Christians contribute to our lives and our walk of faith and so that we might contribute beneficially to *their* lives and *their* walk of faith. If we are to know, experience, and realize God's vision for us, we need to lay aside the value of independence and embrace the New Testament vision for interdependence, each one with each other in the body of Christ, the household of faith.

• Questions for Reflection and Discussion •

Granted that we experience God's presence both in our times of prayer alone and in times of worship in the company of fellow believers, how would you describe the differences, if any, between these two experiences? What dimensions of worship and of encountering God have you discovered in worshiping alongside others that you might not experience in private prayer?

Think about several Christians who have exercised a personal and beneficial impact on your faith formation or your life and who you have seen exercising such impact on the lives of others in the community of believers. How would you and how would the congregation have been diminished without their presence in the body? What have been some of your own contributions to the faith journey and the lives of other believers? How important are we to one another in this life of faith?

Closing Prayer for Session One

Almighty God, your Son redeemed us not to live in splendid isolation but to become one family together in him and to love one another as dearly as our blood relations, for we are all now related by the blood of Jesus. Grant us to grasp more fully the mystery that you have been working out in Christ across centuries and continents—the building of a single, holy temple for your dwelling, the fashioning of a single, well-functioning body—and help us to include ever more fully in our love and care the larger whole of which you have granted us to be parts. We ask this in the name of Jesus, the firstborn of your many sons and daughters. Amen.

2

Welcome One Another

Opening Prayer for Session Two

Give us open ears, O Lord, to hear you speaking to us through your Holy Scriptures and through your holy people, our sisters and brothers. Let us clearly discern what your Holy Spirit would say to us this day and let us be sure to obey so that, in our lives and in our life together, we may ever more fully reflect your good and holy desires for us. We ask this in the name of Jesus, our Lord and Redeemer. Amen.

The welcome we received from Christ is to be reflected, imitated, and extended in the welcome we give to all who have been welcomed by Christ. Christ did not simply "come into my life." He welcomed me into *his* life along with "a great multitude that no one could count, from every nation, from all tribes and peoples and languages" (Rev. 7:9). I did not simply accept Jesus as my Lord and Savior. *Jesus accepted me into his body*, the family of the many sons and daughters adopted along with me into God's household.

The first Christians' willingness to "welcome one another … just as Christ has welcomed you" (Rom. 15:7) stood at the very foundations of the formation and the growth of the early church. Throughout the New Testament, we read about Christians gathering in the homes of the brothers and sisters who had sufficient dwellings to accommodate assemblies as large as perhaps thirty people. In Paul's letters, for example, we learn that Aquila and Prisca (Priscilla) opened their home to a regular assembly of believers in both Ephesus (1 Cor. 16:19) and, later, Rome (Rom. 16:3–5). Nympha hosted a regular assembly in Laodicea (Col. 4:15) and Philemon, in all probability, in Colossae (Philem. 1–2). Gaius was host to "the whole church" in Corinth (Rom. 16:23), which also suggests that smaller circles of Christians in Corinth also met separately in the midsized homes of other believers there (perhaps those of householders like Chloe and Stephanas).

Without the willingness of Christians to welcome one another into their homes, the believers would have had no place to meet, no place to grow, no base for outreach, no matrix for mutual support. Welcoming one another—showing hospitality by opening up one's home to one's sisters and brothers—was the starting point for discovering and nurturing Christian community. This is no doubt why early Christian leaders kept promoting the virtue of the practice of extending hospitality (Rom. 12:13; Heb. 13:2; 1 Peter 4:9). Christian leaders and delegates who traveled from city to city also were welcomed in the home of a local Christian householder. Paul opens a window into this practice when he tells Philemon to prepare a guest room for him, since he hopes to travel back to the region of Asia Minor after his release from the prison where he met Onesimus (Philem. 22). The third letter of John also reflects the practice of traveling Christian teachers needing hospitality (5–8).

Meeting in homes could not help but exercise a formative impact on the ethos of the early Christians, reinforcing their identity as household and family one to another. The welcome that early Christians found in the homes of their new family in Christ—whether in their own city or as they traveled across the cities of the Mediterranean—was one important way in which Christians made Jesus' promise real for one another:

> "Truly I tell you, there is no one who has left house or brothers or sisters or mother or father or children or fields, for my sake and for the sake of the good news, who will not receive a hundredfold now in

this age—houses, brothers and sisters, mothers and children, and fields, with persecutions—and in the age to come eternal life." (Mark 10:29–30; see also Matt. 19:29; Luke 18:29–30)

A group of perhaps ten to fifteen Christians meeting regularly to worship and to touch base in the home of an artisan couple like Aquila and Prisca, or a group as large as twenty-five to thirty meeting regularly in the home of a more elite convert, enjoyed the possibility of really knowing one another and doing life together throughout the week in a manner that was intentionally nurturing of holiness and perseverance, providing the mutual personal support and assistance that facilitates this goal.

• Questions for Reflection and Discussion •

When have relationships with other Christians gone deeper in your experience? What effect did this deepening have on your own life and your commitment to discipleship? What effects did it have on the other believer or believers?

What has been your experience of meeting together with other Christians in homes? In what ways were the dynamics different from meetings in church buildings? What did the setting facilitate better, if anything?

• • •

But *who* is welcome? And to what extent are *these* sisters and brothers in Christ welcome as opposed to *those* sisters and brothers? These were questions with which the early churches had to wrestle—and often far more openly and honestly than we, who still struggle with these questions, acknowledge and wrestle with today. In the first decades of the Christian movement, these questions were bound up with questions of identity, particularly for Jews who came to faith in Christ. What impact, if any, should coming to faith in Christ have on the practices by which Jews continued to preserve their distinctive identity—practices that often meant observing some clear boundaries between themselves and Gentiles, people of any other ethnic group outside their own. Paul opens a window on this issue in his letter to his converts in Galatia. He tells of an episode that had happened in Syrian Antioch that caused quite a stir (Gal. 2:11–14).

A fundamental setting for hospitality in the ancient world—both offering it as a host and accepting it as a guest—was a meal. People who shared a meal at the same table established a deeper level of fellowship with one another and showed a deeper level of acceptance, a willingness to let down the walls. Paul and Barnabas believed that the walls between Jews and Gentiles had been broken down in Christ, and so the Jews and Gentiles among their converts to the faith welcomed one another to their tables in their homes. This becomes even more important when one recalls that the celebration of the Lord's Supper would have taken place in the context of such a fellowship meal (rather than isolated in the worship service in the passing of Styrofoam wafers and tiny individual shot glasses of grape juice). Christ and the ritual of the covenant that he instituted brought Jew and Gentile together at the table.

Peter could go along with this and, in fact, did during his visit to see the work of God among Paul and Barnabas's converts in Antioch. Not all Jewish Christians, however, *could* go along with this. Indeed, a powerful lobby in the early church insisted that Jews were not released from their covenant obligations to observe the walls that God had built around them, to keep them "distinct" from the other nations and "holy" to himself (Acts 15:1–5). It appears to have been quite common for Jews not to eat with Gentiles at all (Acts 10:24; 11:3). But if law-observant Jews *were* willing to do so, they would observe some careful protocols. For example, some Jews, when eating with a Gentile, took the precaution of arranging for there to be a side table on which to rest the pitcher of wine from which they would drink. In this way, if the Gentile guest were to pour a libation to his gods, the Jewish host would not be polluted but the idolatrous action. (It would be rarer for a pious Jew to be willing to go as a guest to a Gentile's house.)

When some Jewish Christians with this mindset came to Antioch from the Jerusalem church, Peter's behavior and that of the Jewish Christians in Antioch changed dramatically. We do not know if they corrected Peter's behavior or if Peter, knowing their mind, simply adjusted once they arrived to avoid being called out by them. What we do know is that:

> When Cephas came to Antioch, I opposed him to his face, because he stood self-condemned; for until certain people came from James, he used to eat with the Gentiles. But after they came, he drew back and kept himself separate for fear of the circumcision faction. And the other Jews joined him in this hypocrisy, so that even Barnabas was led astray by their hypocrisy. (Gal. 2:11–13)

Peter, Barnabas, and the other Jewish Christians of Antioch found themselves caught between the expectations of the Jewish Christians of Jerusalem (Jews are to maintain their separateness when it comes to eating with Gentiles and, thus, preserve their purity and their identity) and their own convictions (the Christ who gave his Holy Spirit to both Jew and Gentile and made us one family together would have us reflect that unity at the family table). Choosing to live in line with expectations as opposed to convictions led Paul to make the charge that they were play-acting (the sense of hypocrisy). Paul believes that what they *ought* to have done would have been to continue to live out their bold witness to what Christ had really accomplished in the world, welcoming both Jew and Gentile to his table and, thus, necessitating that they welcome one another at the table.

Paul is also deeply concerned about the impact of this practice upon the Gentile Christians in Antioch. They had believed (and had partly come to experience) that Christ really had torn down the wall that separated Jew from Gentile. They had also been willing to leave behind their own anti-Jewish prejudices (which were aggressively fostered in Greek and Roman culture) to embrace that truth along with their new Jewish Christian sisters and brothers. Now they witnessed those Jewish Christian sisters and brothers changing their practice, reorganizing church life so that Jewish Christians were no longer sharing table fellowship with Gentile Christians. This, no doubt, required a shift in the practice of how the believers in Antioch assembled— the Jewish Christians now gathering in one or more Jewish Christians' homes, the Gentile Christians now meeting separately in one or more Gentile Christians' homes. Paul feared that, as a result, the Gentile Christians would come to believe that they needed to make themselves Jews in order to be welcomed again. Or perhaps the result would be two separate but equal Christian movements in Antioch. Thus, Paul had to speak up and confront Peter.

Paul only recounted this episode in Galatians because rival Jewish-Christian teachers had made their way to Galatia in an attempt to correct Paul's preaching of the gospel there. They began to teach Paul's Galatian converts that only those Gentiles who accept circumcision and take on a law-observant lifestyle—that is, who make themselves Jews—are truly and fully welcomed into the family of Abraham and the family of God. In his response, Paul declares that what God had accomplished in Christ had far greater implications for *every* line that had been drawn through humanity than the rival teachers realized:

> In Christ Jesus you are all children of God through faith. As many of you as were baptized into Christ have clothed yourselves with Christ. There is no longer Jew or Greek, there is no longer slave or free, there is no longer male and female; for all of you are one in Christ Jesus. (Gal. 3:26–28)

Human societies draw a lot of lines between people. To define an "us," they require a "them," whether the Jews who define themselves over against the Gentiles or the Greeks who define themselves over against the barbarians. Many of the lines drawn result in an "us" that enjoy considerably greater privilege and power than the corresponding "them"—the privilege of being a Jew rather than a Gentile in the Temple State of Israel, the privilege of being a Greek rather than a barbarian in the Hellenistic kingdoms prior to the rise of Rome, the privilege of being male rather than female or a free person rather than a slave in *any* of these settings. Paul declares all such lines to have been rendered valueless now for those who have been immersed into Christ, in whom all have become sons and daughters in the family of God and are to be valued and welcomed by one another on that basis.

A decade later, Paul would return to this topic as he wrote to Christians in and around Ephesus, where he had spent several years himself and where several members of his missionary team had made progress planting churches on their own:

> For he is our peace; in his flesh he has made both groups into one and has broken down the dividing wall, that is, the hostility between us. He has abolished the law with its commandments and ordi-nances, that he might create in himself one new humanity in place of the two, thus making peace, and might reconcile both groups to God in one body through the cross, thus putting to death that hostility through it. (Eph. 2:14–16)

It was imperative to Paul that local Christian assemblies—those groups meeting in houses throughout the eastern half

of the Mediterranean by the time he writes his last letters—
live out this truth, making their practice of welcoming one
another across these lines a living witness to what Christ had
done to these lines. As Paul wrote in his climactic exhortation to the Christians in Rome, again addressing Jewish and
Gentile Christians and their manner of relating: "Welcome
one another, therefore, just as Christ has welcomed you, for
the glory of God" (Rom. 15:7).

While Paul was largely preoccupied with the line that
other Christians wanted to continue to draw between
Jew and Gentile in Christ, he also addressed some other
lines. He consistently pushed his converts to cease to
think of each other in terms of the divisive lines the world
had drawn and to both think of and treat one another in
terms of the new lines God had drawn around all of them
together as brothers and sisters in Christ. The relationship of Philemon, a Colossian Christian householder, and
Onesimus, a slave whom Philemon "owned," provides an
excellent example. Onesimus had somehow not come to the
faith under Philemon's roof, but he did during his separation
from Philemon while in Paul's company (Philem. 10). Now
Paul sends Onesimus to Philemon with the challenge that
Philemon welcome Onesimus on terms entirely different
from those that the world had laid out for their relationship:
"Perhaps this is the reason he was separated from you for a
while, so that you might have him back forever, no longer as

a slave but more than a slave, a beloved brother—especially to me but how much more to you, both in the flesh and in the Lord" (15–16).

Christ's welcome of us into the family of God changes our relationships with one another and the very basis on which we must welcome one another. Outside of Christ, Philemon and Onesimus were positioned to relate to one another as master and slave to Philemon's advantage and Onesimus's detriment. Their shared welcome by Christ into God's family must change all of that—or else that welcome is not real in Philemon's household at all!

• **Questions for Reflection, Discussion, and Action** •

Thinking both in terms of visitors and in terms of people who have been coming for some time: Who receives a warm and honoring welcome in your congregation? Who is greeted with a cooler welcome, or perhaps even disapproval? With whom would you try to avoid sitting at a potluck? What kinds of prejudice—ethnic, economic, cultural, or even as superficial as attire or appearance—are operative in terms of who welcomes whom into the life of your church?

What steps can you take, starting with your own heart and practices, to offer the kind of welcome that reflects a person's value as a part of God's family rather than as an "other" whom society has taught you to value less?

• • •

But on whose terms, then, are we to welcome one another? This was a matter on which Paul had to give some pointed guidance in his letters to the Christians in Corinth and in Rome. In Corinth, a number of Christians saw nothing wrong with buying meat in the marketplace that came from animals that had been sacrificed to the gods in the local temples. Their knowledge that idols were meaningless gave them, they believed, the right to enjoy the meat. Other Christians in Corinth remained scrupulous concerning the spiritual power of idols and, by extension, of the meat that had been spiritually tainted by being associated with the worship of an idol. Since the former considered the latter Christians weak, there was some social pressure upon the weak to show greater spiritual fortitude. One can imagine that this posed some problems, specifically, for the fellowship meal in the homes of the Christian hosts of the churches. Should the welcome be offered on the terms of the strong in Corinth, so that they could enjoy their rights to what they believed their consciences to allow them?

Paul urged against this. While he himself agreed with the position of the strong (as long as they did not go so far as to frequent the fellowship halls of the local pagan temples, to enjoy *their* hospitality), he urged consideration toward the weak. He urged the strong to make room for the scruples of the weak, so as not to cause them spiritual harm—all the more as the strong were no better off in any spiritual sense for eating the meat and no worse off for abstaining (1 Cor. 8:9–13). Rather than insisting on their rights or their liberties, they were to "not seek [their] own advantage, but that of the other" (1 Cor. 10:24). They were to consider their impact on the other person and prioritize providing the kind of environment that would be most hospitable to him or her.

Paul was aware of similar issues among the Roman Christians: "Some believe in eating anything, while the weak eat only vegetables. . . . Some judge one day to be better than another, while others judge all days to be alike" (Rom. 14:2, 5). The issue of eating is similar to what he had encountered in Corinth. The second issue probably reflects the Jewish Christian's observance of the Jewish Sabbath and the Gentile Christian's not making a distinction between six days of work and a seventh day of rest—something that would never have been an identity marker for him or her. The challenge that Paul identifies for them is that God's welcome of each of them, typically evidenced for Paul by their shared reception of the Holy Spirit (Gal. 3:2–5), calls for a broad welcome of each other—together with each other's very different ways of honoring the Lord who redeemed them: "Those who eat must not despise those who abstain, and those who abstain must not pass judgment on those who eat; for God has welcomed them" (Rom. 14:3). In a great many such matters, it is not the practice itself but the heart for God behind the practice that has value. In all such things, we are to make room for one another's practices, once again prioritizing what will secure the *other* person's spiritual well-being within the community of faith (Rom. 14:12–22).

Our welcome of one another has to be sensitive in other dimensions as well. Some of the Corinthian Christians were practicing the common meal which was also the context for the Lord's Supper in ways that, far from providing a genuine welcome, humiliated the poorer members of the community by reminding them of their "lesser" status (1 Cor. 11:17–22). The host or hosts might have been following the standard social practice for large dinner parties, according to which better fare and larger quantities were offered to the guests of similarly high social status while the rest got some bread, wine, and perhaps some olives and cheese. Or the more elite, who did not work regular hours, were able to get started early, leaving insufficient quantities for the laborers and the slaves who would only show up after sunset. Whatever the scenario, the welcome served only to underscore social divisions rather than promote the equality of the members of the family of God. Those failing to welcome the poorer members in a way that showed their equal value in the family risked dishonoring "the body and blood of the Lord" (1 Cor. 11:27) and stood in danger of nothing less than "condemnation" (1 Cor. 11:34).

• Questions for Reflection, Discussion, and Action •

What are some of the unwritten rules by which you and other members of your congregation operate and expect others to operate? When have you seen these rules cause people to withhold the welcome and the affirmation of love and value that we are called to give to one another?

Where do we ourselves need, and where do we need to help particular sisters and brothers see their need, to make greater room for practices that transgress our rules but not God's rules? What steps can you take to move yourself and others in a positive direction in this regard?

Closing Prayer for Session Two

Lord Jesus, you have welcomed us into your family where, to experience your welcome fully, we must welcome one another. Help us, private and guarded as we are, to make room for one another in our hearts, our homes, and our lives, and to permit nothing to shut out again the sisters and brothers you have given us. Teach us the virtue of hospitality—to attend more fully to our guests' feelings than to our rules and customs, and above all, to honor you who welcome to your table all who would come to you. Give us the courage to cross uncomfortable boundaries so that we may both offer to others the welcome you would give them and experience the fellowship that you, and you alone, make possible. We ask this in your name. Amen.

3

Live Harmoniously
with One Another

Opening Prayer for Session Three

Give us open ears, O Lord, to hear you speaking to us through your Holy Scriptures and through your holy people, our sisters and brothers. Let us clearly discern what your Holy Spirit would say to us this day and let us be sure to obey so that, in our lives and in our life together, we may ever more fully reflect your good and holy desires for us. We ask this in the name of Jesus, our Lord and Redeemer. Amen.

Churches do not have a strong reputation for exhibiting harmony among their members. Indeed, the common caricature of a church is that it is full of people who tend to bicker over the most superficial of matters ("Can you believe the committee wants to install *blue* carpet in place of the *red* carpet?"), to jealously defend their turf ("The eleven o'clock service has always been the *traditional* service, and you're *not* going to change that!") or their preferences ("We like to rock it at our contemporary service, so stop trying to introduce those revamped old hymns!"), and to safeguard their own activities or ministries against any competition ("We always have the Men's Yard Sale on the second weekend of October, so you'll have to reschedule your youth retreat or stay out of Fellowship Hall and the lobby area!"). For some congregations, this portrait might be closer to a reflection in a mirror than a caricature. To the extent that this is the case, a church's culture will need a significant overhaul if it is to reflect the New Testament writers' vision for our life together in Christian community.

Paul gives a great deal of attention throughout his letters to shaping the culture or the ethos of Christian communities. When he writes about the kind of conduct—especially the kind of interpersonal conduct—that most appropriately matches up with the love and favor that God has shown us in Christ, he sets living harmoniously with one another front and center:

> Live your life in a manner worthy of the gospel of Christ . . . standing firm in one spirit, striving side by side with one mind for the faith of the gospel. (Phil. 1:27)

> I therefore, the prisoner in the Lord, beg you to lead a life worthy of the calling to which you have been called, with all humility and gentleness, with patience, bearing with one another in love, making every effort to maintain the unity of the Spirit in the bond of peace. There is one body and one Spirit, just as you were called to the one hope of your calling, one Lord, one faith, one baptism, one God and Father of all, who is above all and through all and in all. (Eph. 4:1–6)

Paul's rationale for promoting harmony in Philippians is that the real battle to be fought is not against one another, but against their neighbors' attempts to dissuade the Christian converts from continuing in their antisocial and unpatriotic religious commitments. In a world where the civic-minded person worshiped the emperor, refusing to do so and worshiping an executed Judean rebel as king instead raised more than eyebrows. In light of this, the converts could not afford to feed strife with each other; they needed to support one another wholeheartedly in their commitment to their new life in Christ and to strive together to that end.

Paul's rationale in Ephesians is even more fully developed. Indeed, the entire first half of that sermon-in-the-form-of-a-letter lays a deep foundation for this exhortation. He celebrates—and causes his hearers to savor the remembrance of—God's reconciling work in Christ, overcoming each person's alienation from him and each people group's alienation from one another, uniting people across significant differences into one family that is also one body, made alive together by virtue of being animated by one and the same Spirit. He recalls how they—how we—have been invited together, entirely apart from the merit of any of us, to journey toward a grand, eternal destiny together. And the first thing Paul highlights as the response that we might appropriately make in return for God's lavish generosity toward us? Preserving the unity of the body, the family, that God has brought together at such cost to God's own self. As soon as the exhortation is out of Paul's mouth and set down on the parchment, he returns to all the things that bind his hearers together—the "one body and one Spirit," the "one hope of your calling, one Lord, one faith, one baptism, one God and Father of all," urging believers to find, in all of these "ones," sufficient motivation to hold fast to "one another."

Paul sets a high priority on maintaining unity and harmony, telling Christ-followers to "make every effort" to this end. He sets living harmoniously with one another before us as a goal to be achieved and maintained in and through all our interactions with one another, a goal worthy of our first and best efforts. This suggests that we, throughout our Christian communities, need to nurture a culture that is very different from the culture of competition and the calculus of winning versus losing (that is, where someone's victory comes at the cost of another person's defeat) in the society around us. Seeing ourselves in competition with other people has become almost instinctive, adversely shaping interactions among Christian sisters and brothers.

We need to shift away from an ethos of competition to an ethos of cooperation. This is precisely what ancient ethicists said that natural brothers and sisters needed to do as well. Plutarch, born around the time Paul was writing his first letters, wrote that brothers and sisters needed "to resist the spirit of contentiousness and jealousy . . . when it first creeps in over trivial matters, practicing the art of making mutual concessions, of learning to take defeat, and of taking pleasure in indulging brothers rather than in winning victories over them."[1] He claimed that Nature provided a person with

---

1. Plutarch, "On Fraternal Affection" (17) in *Moralia*, 488a. The translation is from Plutarch, *Moralia. Volume 6* (translated by W. C. Helmbold; Loeb Classical Library; Cambridge, MA: Harvard University Press, 1939), 301.

brothers and sisters "not for difference and opposition to each other, but that by being separate they might the more readily co-operate with one another,"[2] even as the several fingers of a hand work together to accomplish some task. Working against a brother or sister's interests and advantage is as unnatural and dysfunctional as for one hand to break what the other hand has built or for one foot to seek to trip up the other.

It is precisely this kinship ethic that Paul and other early Christian leaders tap into as they urge those whom Christ has made brothers and sisters to "live in harmony with one another" (Rom. 12:16) and to "be of the same mind" (Phil. 2:2; 4:2). I myself prefer to translate this latter phrase, "come to agreement with one another," since Paul himself presumes that there will be times of disagreement and discussion. What concerns him is that disagreement should not move in the direction of disgruntlement, discord, and dislike, but rather in the direction of discernment of a united path forward. Paul gives several specific instructions that would serve to facilitate this transformation. Writing to the congregation in Philippi—a congregation that had been a

---

2. Plutarch, "On Fraternal Affection," (2) 478e. The translation is from Plutarch, *Moralia. Volume 6* (translated by W. C. Helmbold; Loeb Classical Library; Cambridge, MA: Harvard University Press, 1939), 251.

good partner to Paul in his labors and that now faces some internal dissension—Paul instructs them to: "Do nothing from selfish ambition or conceit, but in humility regard others as better than yourselves. Let each of you look not to your own interests, but to the interests of others. Let the same mind be in you that was in Christ Jesus" (Phil. 2:3–5).

He follows this with a remarkable hymnic passage about the mind that was in Christ—the mind and determination that led him to empty himself not only of his divine position and prerogatives but also of the dignity and self-gratification that many human beings might enjoy, "taking the form of a slave" and making himself "obedient to the point of death— even death on a cross" (Phil. 2:7–8).

Our interactions with one another provide us with an endless string of opportunities to allow the mind of Christ to take shape in us and even become more instinctive to us than the instincts of competition and self-assertion nurtured in us by our society. If we were more concerned to win this internal battle—resulting in our own sanctification!—we would quite easily maintain the bond of unity. As Jesus did not look out for what was in his own interests, but invested himself instead in what was entirely in *our* own interests and *God's* interests for us, so the mind of Christ would lead us to have a greater care for the interests of our sisters and brothers than for our own. How different would that recent council meeting or committee meeting have gone if everyone present were committed to work together to safeguard one another's interests rather than push their own agenda through? How different would some of our ministries look if we were intent on making room for our sisters and brothers to flourish and excel—with our encouragement rather than our envy?

Paul's letter to the Christians in Philippi has so much material in it relevant to nurturing a culture of cooperation and harmony, in part, because two prominent figures in that particular Christian community were at odds with one another and Paul was keen on seeing them repair their relationship. He wrote: "I urge Euodia and I urge Syntyche to be of the same mind in the Lord. Yes, and I ask you also, my loyal companion, help these women, for they have struggled beside me in the work of the gospel" (Phil. 4:2–3).

Paul gives no clues concerning what gave rise to the breach in their relationship. Since he had urged them all to have "the mind of Christ," who *emptied* himself for the sake of accomplishing God's purposes, it is probably not too much of a stretch to suggest that Paul thought Euodia and Syntyche had gotten a bit too full of themselves in the course of their service to the congregation. Since one of God's overriding purposes, however, is that we should live harmoniously with one another, being full of ourselves and serving God's purposes will never go hand in hand. We, too, may need this reminder at some point in our involvement in the life of our congregation, so that we can pause long enough to consider how taking on the mind of Christ and having a genuine care for what is on the heart of a sister or brother would change our interactions in a way that would be God-pleasing.

Paul incidentally indicates here what ought to be the role of third parties (any "true yokefellow" [Phil. 4:3 RSV]) in situations of conflict between two Christians. It is not the role that one typically sees—that of the audience brought in to take sides. Rather, their role is to provide community support—and community pressure—for addressing and resolving the disagreement and disharmony in a healthful direction.

• Questions for Reflection, Discussion, and Action •

Recall one or two situations in your experience of Christian community when things escalated to emotionally charged conflict. To what extent was the conflict fueled by competing concerns or interests that each party believed to be at risk? To what extent was it fueled by other factors? What would it have looked like for each party to adopt the mind of Christ in that situation? Would the relational gains have been worth the procedural costs (like lost time or compromised outcome)?

What conversations are going on in the life of your congregation right now that are leading to individuals or groups taking sides? How could you and others work together to change the dynamics of these conversations such that each party hears and values the concerns of the other and commits to discovering the way forward that honors the other—that is, moves from a stance of competition to one of cooperation?

• • •

Of course, we will not always be mindful of looking out for our brothers' or sisters' interests ahead of our own. We will not always treat our sisters or brothers with the honor and respect that is their due. We *will* inevitably run afoul of one another on occasion, whether it is because we have ridden over a sister or brother in the process of assuring that our own interests or desires prevail, or because we allow our annoyance with our sisters or brothers, rather than our love for them or their value in God's sight, to drive our responses to them from time to time. On occasion, the injuries we inflict upon one another in the body of Christ will be deeper and more serious. If we are to live harmoniously with one another, we need to address these wounds that we inflict on one another in a timely manner, lest bitterness take root in our faith communities and become a more serious obstacle to mutual trust and to "striving side by side with one mind"

(Phil. 1:27). The earliest leaders of the Christian move-ment—beginning with Jesus himself—gave clear guidance concerning forgiving and seeking forgiveness from one another when interpersonal issues went beyond simply "bearing with one another" (Eph. 4:2).

The healthy, resilient, harmonious relationship is not the one that is never breached, but the one where breaches are quickly addressed and repaired, and mutual affection speedily restored. Jesus assigns a high priority to such repair work: "So when you are offering your gift at the altar, if you remember that your brother or sister has something against you, leave your gift there before the altar and go; first be reconciled to your brother or sister, and then come and offer your gift" (Matt. 5:23–24).

The work of reconciliation is sufficiently urgent to inter-rupt our acts of worship in God's house! One can easily imagine the rationale for such urgency: our acts of worship are blemished when grudges and unresolved injuries are on our hearts and interrupting the harmony of the family that Christ died to bring together in one body, filled with one Spirit. Paul is also keen to see Christ-followers making reconciliation a priority. When he advises Christians in and around Ephesus not to "let the sun go down on your anger" (Eph. 4:26), it is likely that he is urging a disciple who has experienced some offense or provocation to deal with the interpersonal rift by taking the initiative to restore the relationship. Paul's advice is reminiscent of the practice of followers of the Greek philosopher Pythagoras who, "if ever they were led by anger into recrimination, never let the sun go down before they joined right hands, embraced each other, and were reconciled."[3]

But Jesus does not lay the obligation of seeking reconciliation only upon the brother or sister who has *given* offense to another member of the community of faith. He also lays this obligation upon the one who has *received* the offense or injury.

> "If another disciple sins, you must rebuke the offender, and if there is repentance, you must forgive. And if the same person sins against you seven times a day, and turns back to you seven times and says, 'I repent,' you must forgive." (Luke 17:3–4)

> "If your brother sins against you, go and tell him his fault, between you and him alone. If he listens to you, you have gained your brother." (Matt. 18:15 ESV)

---

3. Plutarch, "On Fraternal Affection" (17) in *Moralia*, 488b–c. The translation is from Plutarch, *Moralia. Volume 6* (translated by W. C. Helmbold; Loeb Classical Library; Cambridge, MA: Harvard University Press, 1939), 301.

We are not talking here about the inevitable chafing and irritations that occur between people of different temperaments. For such trifles, the admonition to "[bear] with one another in love" (Eph. 4:2) provides sufficient guidance. Here Jesus is speaking about actual offenses, which would appropriately call for repentance as the path to reconciliation. And Jesus gives excellent, practical advice for the person who has been wronged by a sister or brother. It is so much better than the typical, alternative practice—where the person who has experienced some wrong approaches just about anyone else in the congregation and talks about what so-and-so did, arousing ill will toward so-and-so while not doing anything positive to restore the relationship, rather than directly approaching the offending person. Indeed, Jesus' own half-brother, James, strongly cautions Christ-followers against pursuing this destructive, alternative practice:

> Do not speak evil against one another, brothers and sisters. Whoever speaks evil against another or judges another, speaks evil against the law and judges the law. (James 4:11a)

> Beloved, do not grumble against one another, so that you may not be judged. See, the Judge is standing at the doors! (James 5:9)

We have all witnessed (and perhaps even been party to) such grumbling about what some fellow believer did and the way this spread dissension and further eroded harmony. Jesus' advice is far more productive both for the endangered relationship and for the continued health and harmony of the community.

We can never lose sight of the fact that the person with whom we have a temporary relational problem is eternally a brother or a sister! A slave-turned-philosopher named Epictetus, who flourished near the end of the first century, wrote that:

> Everything has two handles, one by which it may be carried and the other not. If your brother acts unjustly toward you, do not take hold of it by this side, that he has acted unjustly (since this is the handle by which it may not be carried), but instead by this side, that he is your brother and was brought up with you, and you will be taking hold of it in the way that it can be carried.[4]

Jesus' instructions are built upon the same wisdom: the person who has injured you in some way or other is, first and foremost, your brother or sister in the Lord—not your

---

4. Epictetus, *Enchiridion* 43. From *Handbook of Epictetus*, trans. Nicholas P. White (Indianapolis: Hackett Publishing Co., 1983), 26.

enemy, even though you may temporarily find yourselves at odds. And as in any family, the context of *being* family sets the goal for confrontation always as the restoration of the relationship and of peace and harmony within the family. The important step of talking to the brother or sister whom you believe to have sinned against you gives the two of you the possibility of identifying a misunderstanding, and thus repairing the damage, or of exchanging needed apologies and forgiveness.

Reconciliation—the seeking and offering of forgiveness—is not just good advice for community; it is Christ's mandate for all who follow him. This mandate is implicitly written into the prayer that, of all prayers, most binds Christians of every age and every place together; namely, the Lord's Prayer. In it, we pray, "forgive us our debts, as we also have forgiven our debtors" (Matt. 6:12), and this is the only petition within the prayer that Jesus is remembered to have commented upon: "For if you forgive others their trespasses, your heavenly Father will also forgive you; but if you do not forgive others, neither will your Father forgive your trespasses" (Matt. 6:14–15). But the logic is ultimately not that I offer forgiveness in order that I might receive forgiveness. It is that we offer forgiveness *because* we have been forgiven—and forgiven by God for far greater offenses against God's honor and righteousness than we will ever be asked to forgive (Matt. 18:23–35). "If anyone has a complaint against another, forgive each other; just as the Lord has forgiven you, so you also must forgive" (Col. 3:13). It is important to remember that we were all forgiven together by God, and that part of God's purpose in forgiving us together was to bring us together into a community of unfailing love and mutual support. Forgiving one another is in line with both God's character and God's purposes.

In my experience, conversations about forgiveness and, indeed, the mandate to forgive almost always turn to the most difficult cases—those instances that, because of the gravity of the injury, seem impossible to forgive. These instances, then, tend to derail the conversation and blunt the force of our Lord's challenge to us. It might be more productive to approach this in a different way. For example, focusing on how many relational burdens we are carrying that we likely can resolve and to think about how to approach and mend those damaged relationships effectively with a view to forgiving and reconciling. This would be true whether we are the ones who have initiated injury or the ones who believe we were ourselves injured.

• Questions for Reflection, Discussion, and Action •

Think about your circles of Christian community. Are there impediments in any of your relationships with these sisters and brothers? For which impediments are you at fault? For which do you think your sister or brother to be at fault? For which is it unclear, or is their shared responsibility?

What steps will you take in the very near future—perhaps even yet today—to approach these sisters and brothers with a view to reconciliation, renewal of harmony, and restoration of the relationship? How can you approach those conversations in a way that will most facilitate that outcome?

Closing Prayer for Session Three

Almighty God, who reconciled us to yourself and to one another at great cost to yourself in your beloved Son, teach us so to value the unity of the Holy Spirit that we will make every effort to maintain that unity in the bond of peace. Help us to be more concerned to safeguard the interests of our sisters and brothers than our own, so that the mind of Christ may surely be formed within us. Help us to value relationships and reconciliation rather than nurse our own injured pride or cherish our grudges, so that we may extend forgiveness to one another as freely as we have received—and will again need—forgiveness from you. We ask all this in the name of Jesus, who is our peace. Amen.

4

Love One Another

Opening Prayer for Session Four

Give us open ears, O Lord, to hear you speaking to us through your Holy Scriptures and through your holy people, our sisters and brothers. Let us clearly discern what your Holy Spirit would say to us this day and let us be sure to obey so that, in our lives and in our life together, we may ever more fully reflect your good and holy desires for us. We ask this in the name of Jesus, our Lord and Redeemer. Amen.

Every year on the Thursday before Easter, Christians in more liturgical churches celebrate Jesus' institution of the Lord's Supper and his giving of a new commandment to his disciples. Indeed, the traditional name for the day—Maundy Thursday—is derived from the Latin word for "commandment": *mandatum.* But even if Maundy Thursday is not a part of your own Christian community's tradition, you will almost certainly be familiar with the *mandatum:*

> "I give you a new commandment, that you love one another. Just as I have loved you, you also should love one another. By this everyone will know that you are my disciples, if you have love for one another." (John 13:34–35)

> "This is my commandment, that you love one another as I have loved you." (John 15:12)

The solemnity of the occasion of Jesus' giving of this commandment—namely, the very night of his arrest that would lead to his crucifixion the next day—underscores the importance of this mandate.

As we think about the people that God has made one family along with us, it is important to recognize that Jesus presents this as a *commandment*—one that is not to be sporadically fulfilled, but is rather to characterize our lives and our life together as Christ-followers. It is not an optional add-on to "accepting Jesus Christ as *my* Lord and Savior," but the ongoing practice that *shows* one to have indeed accepted Jesus Christ as one's Lord and Savior. John explicitly connects the confession of faith and the life of loving the household of faith: "And this is his commandment, that we should believe in the name of his Son Jesus Christ and love one another, just as he has commanded us" (1 John 3:23). Paul, whom many Protestant Christians celebrate as the apostle of the gospel of "faith alone" (even though Paul himself never once writes of "faith alone"), likewise links the faith that counts with a life of loving practice: "the only thing that counts is faith working through love" (Gal. 5:6).

Paul wrote his letter to the Galatians in response to rival teachers who had been claiming that Paul's Gentile converts needed to accept circumcision and adopt a Torah-observant lifestyle—meaning, they needed to become Jewish—in order to be "justified," that is, to fall in line with God's expectations of the person whom God would declare "righteous." In his letter to his converts in Galatia, he warned them that the rival teachers were leading them in a very dangerous direction, for if they decided that they needed to observe the Jewish law after all, they would be issuing a vote of no confidence in Jesus and in the gift that Jesus had procured for them; namely, the Holy Spirit.

By contrast, Paul urged them to continue to believe that Jesus' death and resurrection on their behalf—and the Holy Spirit that had come upon them to guide them and empower them for righteousness before God—were sufficient for the task. It is in this context that he says: "For in Christ

Jesus neither circumcision nor uncircumcision counts for anything; the only thing that counts is faith working through love" (Gal. 5:6). It is significant that Paul did not write: "the only thing that counts is faith," instead describing the quality of the faith that counts: "faith working through love," faith that keeps investing itself in loving action.

Paul did not believe that Jesus died and rose again to excuse people from fulfilling God's righteous vision for their lives. On the contrary, he believed that Jesus died, rose again, and bestowed the Spirit on his followers in order to *empower* them to fulfill that vision. And following Jesus' own elevation of the particular commandment tucked away in Leviticus 19:18—"Love your neighbor as yourself"—as the heart of the law of Moses, Paul likewise understands God's vision for human life and community to be a vision of loving commitment to one another: "For the whole law is summed up in a single commandment, 'You shall love your neighbor as yourself'" (Gal. 5:14).

> Owe no one anything, except to love one another; for the one who loves another has fulfilled the law. The commandments, "You shall not commit adultery; You shall not murder; You shall not steal; You shall not covet"; and any other commandment, are summed up in this word, "Love your neighbor as yourself." Love does no wrong to a neighbor; therefore, love is the fulfilling of the law. (Rom. 13:8–10)

Note that Paul places his emphasis on loving one another, even when Paul has in mind the commandment to love your neighbor as the text undergirding the instruction. Showing Christ's love to the world outside of the church will always be an essential facet of our mission, but there is also a great deal to be said for making our love as fully and pervasively real as possible among our sisters and brothers in Christ—and there is a great deal to be done to make this real not only in our local reach but also in our global reach.

If Jesus commands us to "love one another," he clearly has in mind something other than, and beyond, feeling the emotion of love. As with any other command, this one involves a decision to act. It involves a decision to love, a commitment to love *these* people that God has made my sisters and brothers. It involves the decision to commit to *these* people, to persevere in relationship with them and in working alongside them for *their* good and for the good that God will accomplish through all of you together. Love becomes a catchword for committing to relate to one another in particular ways and to act on one another's behalf in particular ways. In regard to the former, Paul writes:

> Love is patient; love is kind; love is not envious or boastful or arrogant or rude. It does not insist on its own way; it is not irritable or resentful; it does not rejoice in wrongdoing, but rejoices in the truth. It

> bears all things, believes all things, hopes all things,
> endures all things. Love never ends. (1 Cor. 13:4–8a)

I most often hear this passage read at weddings. While it is indeed applicable to that most intimate of relationships between a brother and sister in the Lord, it is not to be romanticized and compartmentalized in the life of the Christian couple. I have also often heard in many a sermon the familiar trope whereby the preacher invites the congregation to read through the passage replacing the word "love" with "God" or "Jesus," since we are told in Scripture that "God is love" (1 John 4:8). But Paul was not trying to say something about God here. Rather, he wanted to give some detailed guidance concerning the spirit in which we are to relate to one another throughout the Christian community. He wanted to provide the diagnostics by which we know we are indeed moving together in the most valuable of spiritual gifts (the love for one another that the Spirit empowers) or by which we are alerted to the need to check ourselves in our attitudes and interactions.

• Questions for Reflection, Discussion, and Action •

How have you kept yourself mindful of Jesus' new commandment in your interactions with other Christ-followers, especially when the interactions are . . . challenging? Can you recall one or more episodes when mindfulness of this commandment repositioned you to respond with greater forbearance and to seek your brother or sister's good in the interaction?

Can you identify one or more recent episodes when greater mindfulness of and attention to Paul's diagnostics of how love does and does not act would have led you to bear yourself differently toward a sister or brother in the faith? Is there repair work to be done in regard to that relationship and, if so, what steps will you take to that end?

• • •

In addition to committing to relate to one another in particular ways, loving one another means acting on one another's behalf:

> How does God's love abide in anyone who has the world's goods and sees a brother or sister in need and yet refuses help? Little children, let us love, not in word or speech, but in truth and action. (1 John 3:17–18)

> If a brother or sister is naked and lacks daily food, and one of you says to them, "Go in peace; keep warm and eat your fill," and yet you do not supply their bodily

> needs, what is the good of that? So faith by itself, if it
> has no works, is dead. (James 2:15–17)

The command to love one another was understood from
the beginning to involve caring for the needy and vulnerable within the Christian community, or else love would be
merely a matter of talking and not something real.

The early Christian communities took this to heart in
stunning ways. The associate of Paul who wrote what we
call the "Letter to the Hebrews" addressed a congregation or
circle of congregations, some of whose members had experienced significant harassment and loss on account of their
commitment to Jesus. When their commitment finally
begins to wane, the author asks them to:

> recall those earlier days when, after you had been
> enlightened, you endured a hard struggle with suffer-
> ings, sometimes being publicly exposed to abuse and
> persecution, and sometimes being partners with
> those so treated. For you had compassion for those
> who were in prison, and you cheerfully accepted the
> plundering of your possessions, knowing that you
> yourselves possessed something better and more
> lasting. (Heb. 10:32–34)

Particularly noteworthy here is the fact that those who
had not come into the public eye or under direct public

pressure came openly to the aid and comfort of those who had been thus singled out. For the sake of showing their love in direct and practical ways, they risked suffering the same negative attention as had befallen their sisters and brothers. They went the distance for one another, even as members of a biological family would be expected to go the distance for one another. The author hopes that, as they recall their former boldness both in terms of showing their commitment to Jesus *and* their solidarity with one another, they will commit afresh to the kinds of mutual, loving support that will enable those most directly targeted by their neighbors and their society to persevere in the faith.

> Let brotherly love continue. Do not let hospitality be neglected, for by this some have entertained angels unawares. Remember prisoners as though you are their fellow prisoners; those who are being mistreated as though you were in their skin. (Heb. 13:1–3, my translation)

The author of Hebrews drives home the importance of making those who have been most marginalized on account of their faith in Christ feel the support of their family in Christ. Indeed, the faithfulness of their family in Christ reinforces their assurance of Christ's own faithfulness to them at their point of greatest need.

It is probably in connection with such a situation that we should hear Jesus' implied exhortation in his vision of the last judgment—which is notably his last public teaching recorded in the Gospel according to Matthew:

> "Then the king will say to those at his right hand, 'Come, you that are blessed by my Father, inherit the kingdom prepared for you from the foundation of the world; for I was hungry and you gave me food, I was thirsty and you gave me something to drink, I was a stranger and you welcomed me, I was naked and you gave me clothing, I was sick and you took care of me, I was in prison and you visited me.' Then the righteous will answer him, 'Lord, when was it that we saw you hungry and gave you food, or thirsty and gave you something to drink? And when was it that we saw you a stranger and welcomed you, or naked and gave you clothing? And when was it that we saw you sick or in prison and visited you?' And the king will answer them, 'Truly I tell you, just as you did it to one of the least of these who are members of my family, you did it to me.'" (25:34–40)

Several suggestions have been made concerning whom Jesus meant to indicate as "the least" of his sisters and brothers. Since Matthew referred earlier to those who were part of the community of Jesus' followers as "brothers and sisters" (Matt. 18:15, 21, 35; 23:8), it seems highly likely that Matthew and his readers would have thought here of the members of the Christian community who found themselves in greatest need and with the least power to help themselves. And many of the circumstances of need described here would have aligned well with the circumstances of Christ-followers who had lost their livelihoods, their place in a home, even their freedom because of their families' and their neighbors' negative responses to their allegiance to Jesus.

These circumstances continue to beset millions of our sisters and brothers in Christ across the globe. In his new commandment, Jesus commends their care and support to as many of us as have the means and the freedom to love them "not in word and speech, but in truth and action" (1 John 3:18).

Of course, we must be mindful of our sisters and brothers far and near, near and far, rather than artificially choose between them, limiting our love and its practical reach. The local Christian community should also be a place where those sisters and brothers who find themselves in need also find the personal support and material resources they need. We have the opportunity not to neglect hospitality when a Christian brother, sister, or entire family find themselves evicted, when a member of God's household finds himself or herself in an abusive natural or legal household, or when

some physical disaster overtakes a home. We have the opportunity to remember the Christian brother or sister who has
run afoul of the law and finds himself or herself in prison,
continuing our relationship with that person to provide
support through the highly non-rehabilitating experience
of prison and thereafter as he or she seeks to find a place in
society once again.

The point is that loving one another must take the form
of contributing in real ways to one another's lives—in practical interventions that make our talk of being family real
in action. This was the distinguishing mark of the Christian
church in its first centuries. Lucian was a Greek writer of
satires in the early second century. He was by no means
appreciative of the Christ "cult" taking root in the cities of
the Roman Empire. Nevertheless, he bears this testimony to
the commitment Christians showed to one another specifically on the basis of their new kinship in Christ: "Their
first lawgiver persuaded them that they are all brothers of
one another. . . . Therefore they despise all things [i.e., material goods] indiscriminately and consider them common
property."[1] About a century later, the Christian teacher
Tertullian is still able to say that "It is mainly the deeds of
a love so noble that lead many to put a brand [i.e., the label

---

1. Lucian, *The Passing of Peregrinus* (13), trans. A. M. Harmon
(Cambridge, MA: Harvard University Press, 1936), 15.

of "Christian"] upon us. 'See,' they say, 'how they love one another.'"[2] Here, too, we see a love that makes itself real—and makes itself apparent to outsiders—in deeds. And it is in these deeds that the non-Christians see the distinctive character of the community gathered in Jesus' name. While we indeed have an important story to tell to the nations, it must be spoken from a community of people who show the impact that story has had on *their* story, and particularly their story *together*. This is as important a facet of Christian witness now as it was in the first three centuries of the church's existence:

> We will see the greater things of the gospel in the world as the greater love of the gospel finds its way into our relationships. . . . The first half of the gospel is about believing in the love of God for the world. The second half of the gospel is about becoming the love of God in and for the world. We stand on this conviction: the world will awaken to the first half of the gospel as the people of God awaken to the second half of the gospel. In a post-Christian world, the content of the gospel will have little impact on

---

2. Tertullian, *Apology* 39.7. Translation from Alexander Roberts and James Donaldson, eds., *The Ante-Nicene Fathers. Volume III* (Buffalo, NY: Christian Literature Publishing Co., 1887), 134–35.

unbelievers if people do not see it actualized in the relationships among its believers.[3]

• Questions for Reflection, Discussion, and Action •

How responsive are you to the needs of your sisters and brothers in Christ? When have you sought opportunities to reach out in love in practical ways? When have you responded from a full heart when an opportunity presented itself to you? When have you talked yourself down from responding as fully as love and the Spirit might have led you?

Of what needs in your local congregation, in your larger local Christian community, and in the global body of Christ are you (or is your study group) presently aware? How would you respond to these particular needs if they arose within your natural family? How would the Spirit move you to respond to these particular needs now among your family in Christ, such that they will experience the reality of Christian love and the family of God?

• • •

_____

3. Mark Benjamin and J. D. Walt, *Discipleship Bands: A Practical Field Guide* (Franklin, TN: Seedbed Publishing, 2018), 7.

If we are to live out Jesus' new commandment more fully—
to the point that our love for one another in the household
of faith becomes our dominant trait and witness—we need
to hear a few more words from John. The first is his warning
that we can never excuse ourselves from obeying this new
commandment while thinking to preserve our private devotion to God:

> Those who say, "I love God," and hate their brothers
> or sisters, are liars; for those who do not love a
> brother or sister whom they have seen, cannot love
> God whom they have not seen. The commandment
> we have from him is this: those who love God must
> love their brothers and sisters also. (1 John 4:20–21)

John's summary of "the commandment we have from
him" clearly recalls Jesus' summary of the Torah—or, better,
Jesus' selection of its two weightiest and most indispensable
commandments:

> "'You shall love the Lord your God with all your heart,
> and with all your soul, and with all your mind.' This
> is the greatest and first commandment. And a second
> is like it: 'You shall love your neighbor as yourself.'"
> (Matt. 22:37–39)

John understands, however, that these two commandments do not merely sit side by side. Rather, they are so

closely intertwined and connected that to fail to obey the one is to fail to obey the other. Our love for God either manifests itself in our love for one another, or our love for God is demonstrated to be a fiction!

Perhaps also realizing how difficult and challenging it would be to maintain our love for one another because we can be so very *unlovable* from time to time, John reminds us of the source and foundation of our love for one another:

> Beloved, let us love one another, because love is from God; everyone who loves is born of God and knows God. Whoever does not love does not know God, for God is love. God's love was revealed among us in this way: God sent his only Son into the world so that we might live through him. In this is love, not that we loved God but that he loved us and sent his Son to be the atoning sacrifice for our sins. Beloved, since God loved us so much, we also ought to love one another. No one has ever seen God; if we love one another, God lives in us, and his love is perfected in us. . . . We love because he first loved us. (1 John 4:7–12, 19)

First, John makes clear that love is not something offered in response to the other party. God showed what love is, not by responding to our devotion, but by loving us while we were alienated and estranged from him, by suffering death in the Word-made-Flesh to reconcile us to himself. This is the species of love that God calls for us to have for one another. Our loving is thus not a reaction to the brother or sister behaving well, that is, in a manner that evokes love; consequently, a brother or sister behaving in an unloving way does not become an excuse for us to respond the same way. Rather, we love one another in response to, and as a consequence of, God's having loved us, so that we offer love to one another independently of how the other may be treating us at any given moment.

Second, it is a consequence of our having been thus loved together by God, of having shared this experience of being loved by God. It is a valuing of the God who loved both me and my brother or sister, so that out of regard for God I love (and persevere in loving) those whom God has so loved. Loving God's family is the sign that one has been "born of God" into that new family. Plutarch would write around the turn of the first century that loving one's brothers and sisters offers "a proof of love for both mother and father."[4] John may have something like this in mind here when he cites God's loving us as the reason "we also ought to love one

---

4. Plutarch, "On Fraternal Affection" (6) in *Moralia*, 480f. The translation is from Plutarch, *Moralia. Volume 6* (translated by W. C. Helmbold; Loeb Classical Library; Cambridge, MA: Harvard University Press, 1939), 261.

another" (1 John 4:11); without such love for one another, we do not show God the love God merits (1 John 4:20–21).

Finally, loving one another—in imitation of God, who loved us first—shows each member of the household of faith to have been "born of God." Children were held to reflect the character of their parents and, if God is indeed love itself, those who have genuinely been born of God will show that family resemblance: "everyone who loves is born of God" (1 John 4:7). Paul draws upon this cultural logic as well when he urges the Christians in and around Ephesus to "be imitators of God, as beloved children, and live in love, as Christ loved us and gave himself up for us, a fragrant offering and sacrifice to God" (Eph. 5:1–2). The character of the Father, most brilliantly displayed in the eternal Son, will also take root and bear fruit in the lives of the many sons and daughters.

• Questions for Reflection, Discussion, and Action •

When has your experience of knowing God's love for and commitment to you empowered you to love your sisters and brothers more fully and with greater commitment?

If God were to assess your love for him based on the love that you have shown your sisters and brothers in his family this past week or month, what would that assessment be?

What would it look like for you to love particular sisters or brothers, near or far, with the love that God showed us in sending his Son on our behalf? If you are not already living at the level of showing such love, what do you need in order to do so to a greater degree?

Closing Prayer for Session Four

Lord Jesus, you have commanded us to love the members of the family that you have given us, and you have shown us what the full measure of that love is to be. Open our eyes to the needs of our sisters and brothers at home and abroad; open our minds to the ways, both simple and creative, in which we can reach out to them in love; and open our hearts so that we love as you have loved, without holding ourselves back from doing what is right and pleasing in your sight. Let our commitment to you—our faith—become effective through love, so that, in our embrace and support of our sisters and brothers, we return to you the love that we owe. And let our constant practice of such love change our own hearts till we also embody the love that is your very essence. In your name we pray. Amen.

5

Serve One Another

Opening Prayer for Session Five

Give us open ears, O Lord, to hear you speaking to us through your Holy Scriptures and through your holy people, our sisters and brothers. Let us clearly discern what your Holy Spirit would say to us this day and let us be sure to obey so that, in our lives and in our life together, we may ever more fully reflect your good and holy desires for us. We ask this in the name of Jesus, our Lord and Redeemer. Amen.

The four Gospels are unanimous in their witness to Jesus' teaching that genuine discipleship involves genuine service from a genuine servant's heart. This was the character of Jesus' own heart, and it will be reproduced in those who genuinely follow him. On one occasion on the way to Jerusalem, James and John—who along with Peter formed the inner core of Jesus' disciples—asked Jesus to grant them the places of greatest authority and status alongside him. Jesus replied to them and all who were present to hear:

> "You know that among the Gentiles those whom they recognize as their rulers lord it over them, and their great ones are tyrants over them. But it is not so among you; but whoever wishes to become great among you must be your servant, and whoever wishes to be first among you must be slave of all. For the Son of Man came not to be served but to serve, and to give his life a ransom for many." (Mark 10:42–45; see also Matt. 20:25–28; Luke 22:25–27)

In the upside-down kingdom that Jesus came to establish, bending down to serve is the activity of the great ones, while refraining from stooping down to lift up a brother or sister because it's beneath one characterizes the nobodies in the kingdom. This kind of talk would be absurd were it not for the activity of the Lord of the kingdom, who came not to be served (as most lords would expect and enforce), but to offer service—and to put himself out for others to the extent of giving himself over to be nailed to a cross and die for them.

John does not record this particular episode and teaching moment in his Gospel. He does show this very word, however, taking on flesh in a stunning manner. We find ourselves back at Maundy Thursday, which also commemorates Jesus washing his disciples' feet. On the night that Jesus gave his disciples his new commandment, that we should love one another, he first demonstrated for his disciples how love—real love such as Jesus himself showed—means serving one another. Providing water and a basin for rinsing off the sand and grit from sandal-clad feet was a standard act of hospitality in the ancient Mediterranean. It was always performed by social inferiors on behalf of social superiors— slaves for masters and their guests, children for parents, wives for husbands, even disciples for rabbis. In the status-conscious world of the Roman Empire, one would not see social superiors performing this task for juniors.

Jesus' violation of these norms must have made the disciples extremely uncomfortable, even embarrassed. It affronted them to the extent that Peter sought to opt out of this particular social experiment: "You will never wash my feet" (John 13:8). But Jesus insisted that Peter allow him, or else Peter would have no part in the community Jesus was creating, the *kingdom* Jesus was initiating. Why? Peter's refusal was an affirmation of what was proper within the world's hierarchy of who serves whom, and there's no room for that to be affirmed in Jesus' family. For Peter to allow

Jesus to wash his feet—to participate in this status-smashing act—was to have his own orientation permanently changed. The New Revised Standard Version captures this well in its rendering of the question that Jesus asks once he has completed the rounds: "Do you know what I have done to you?" (John 13:12). The question is ambiguous in the Greek. The last phrase could be read either "for you" or "to you." But Jesus has not just done something *for* the Twelve; he has done something *to* them. He has laid a challenge before them, an obligation upon them:

> "You call me Teacher and Lord—and you are right, for that is what I am. So if I, your Lord and Teacher, have washed your feet, you also ought to wash one another's feet. For I have set you an example, that you also should do as I have done to you. Very truly, I tell you, servants are not greater than their master, nor are messengers greater than the one who sent them. If you know these things, you are blessed if you do them." (John 13:13–17)

Having seen that the menial task of washing the feet of the guests of a household is not beneath their Lord, they know that it is not beneath them to do so as well. But, of course, Jesus is about to go further. If laying down his life for his disciples and for those who would come to believe through their testimony was not beneath him, laying down their lives for one another was not beneath them either. Laying down *our* lives for one another is also not beneath us. Indeed, it is the highwater mark to which we must aspire.

• Questions for Reflection and Discussion •

Who exhibits a servant's heart among the people in your congregation or among those in some other of your circles? How does this manifest itself?

What leaders in your church or perhaps even in a secular institution exhibit a servant's heart? How does this manifest itself? What impact, if any, does it have on the culture of the institution?

In what settings have you exhibited a servant's heart? How available do you make yourself to serve the needs of, or otherwise come alongside and assist, your sisters and brothers in the faith? When have you held back from serving because you felt some task was beneath you?

• • •

Loving one another and serving one another are inextricably bound. It is by means of the latter that we make the former real, that love takes on flesh in deeds. Jesus himself is remembered to have made this connection:

> "This is my commandment, that you love one another as I have loved you. No one has greater love than this, to lay down one's life for one's friends.... I am giving you these commands so that you may love one another." (John 15:12–13, 17)

John made the connection even more explicit:

> For this is the message you have heard from the beginning, that we should love one another.... We know love by this, that he laid down his life for us— and we ought to lay down our lives for one another. (1 John 3:11, 16)

Jesus expressed his love for his disciples by laying down his life for them; his followers are called to love one another by doing the same. In most contexts, however, laying down our lives for one another does not mean dying for one another; rather, it means *living* for one another, putting ourselves out there to serve them for their good (as opposed to living for ourselves, seeking our own good).

The apostle Paul also perceived that love becomes real through serving—and that such love-through-serving fulfills

the very purpose for which Christ liberated us from our
former slavery to the "fundamental principles of the world"
(Gal. 4:3, my translation), such as the hierarchies of who
should serve whom that Jesus himself turned upside down:

> For you were called to freedom, brothers and sisters;
> only do not use your freedom as an opportunity for
> self-indulgence, but through love become slaves to
> one another. For the whole law is summed up in a
> single commandment, "You shall love your neighbor
> as yourself." (Gal. 5:13–14)

Paul has just spent several chapters in this letter urging
his converts in Galatia to preserve the freedom that Christ
won for them at such great cost to himself—freedom
from living inside the lines that their society had drawn
for them, freedom even from living inside the lines that
God had drawn for historic Israel in the law of Moses.
This freedom, however, is not license. We have not been
cut loose from the domination of the world, the flesh, and
the devil to pursue our own interests and our own self-
realization. Rather, we have been given freedom so that
we might voluntarily offer ourselves in service first and
foremost to one another in the Christian community—
locally and beyond. We have been given the freedom
to let the mind of Christ come to life within us and take
us over, the mind of the one who "came not to be served,

but to serve" (Mark 10:45). This freedom drives us to seek for opportunities to serve in Jesus' name, not to indulge ourselves in the name of our rights.

Paul uses a particularly bold metaphor in this passage. Perhaps out of sensitivity to the devastating and ongoing effects of chattel slavery as an institution in the United States into the nineteenth century, many translations soft-pedal this image. The NIV, for example, reads: "serve one another humbly in love" (Gal. 5:13). Paul, however, chooses a verb that contains the image of "serving *as slaves*." Paul could easily have chosen a different verb that lacked this connotation, but instead he used the verb that suggests that we are ultimately bound to one another—and bound to one another as those who must take up the towel and the basin for one another. In one sense, we choose to accept the call to serve one another; but in another sense, we are reminded that our Lord purchased us: "You are not your own, for you were bought with a price" (1 Cor. 6:19–20 ESV). And he that purchased us commands us both to "love one another" (John 13:34) and to lay down our lives for one another (John 15:12–13)—again, generally not in a single day's act of martyrdom, but in the daily dying to one's own interests and agenda so that the mind of Christ might become operative in us in service to one another. It is in this way that Christ takes shape among us, as Paul passionately summed up the goal of his work on behalf of his congregations (Gal. 4:19).

There are many opportunities to cultivate a servant's heart in our life together in the local congregation. Every time that you or someone around you notices something that somebody ought to be doing presents such an opportunity, especially if your first reaction is that it's beneath you. Should the custodian have emptied the garbage in the narthex or fellowship hall before Sunday morning? Should the ushers have picked up the sanctuary better? Should the visitation team be doing a better job getting out to visit more shut-ins or hospitalized parishioners? Should the trustees be getting things fixed in a more timely way? You get the idea. If you find yourself picking up a basin and a towel a bit more frequently, it only means you're making positive progress toward Christ-likeness.

Taking up a towel for one another is an essential training exercise in discipleship. But Jesus calls us to do much more. He calls us to take up a cross for one another, laying aside our own pursuits, our own delights, our own time and resources for the sake of meeting the very real needs of the sisters and brothers both in our midst and throughout the globe. He calls us to lavish upon those most in need among Jesus' family the love and investment of ourselves that Jesus lavished upon

us. The author of the Letter to the Hebrews urges us to accept
this call as, simply, the right thing to do:

> Ground that drinks up the rain falling on it repeat-
> edly, and that produces a crop useful to those for
> whom it is cultivated, receives a blessing from
> God. . . . God is not unjust; he will not overlook your
> work and the love that you showed for his sake in
> serving the saints, as you still do. And we want each
> one of you to show the same diligence so as to realize
> the full assurance of hope to the very end, so that you
> may not become sluggish, but imitators of those who
> through faith and patience inherit the promises.
> (6:7, 10–12)

Having spent chapters enumerating the many benefits
that God has bestowed on us in Christ, the writer calls us
to prove ourselves honorable recipients of these gifts by
making the kind of return that would please the giver. Just
as good ground soaking up the gifts of rain after rain eventually yields a good crop for those on whose behalf the ground
was being cultivated, so we are called to yield a good crop
for those on whose behalf God has been cultivating us—our
sisters and brothers in Christ. Showing our love for them
through service also holds further promise for *us*, since "God
is not unjust" so as to overlook the fact that God's generosity
toward us has borne good fruit. Laying ourselves aside and

living for one another proves to be the best investment in our own future that we can make, for it is the response to God's many favors that, by honoring God's generosity, most assures that we will encounter favor in the future when we stand before God to give an account of how we have used God's grace.

In order to offer ourselves in service to our sisters and brothers in their need, however, we need to see what their needs are. The author of Hebrews, recognizing this, urges:

> Let us look closely at one another with the result that love and good deeds burst forth, not neglecting our assembling together (as is the habit for some), but encouraging one another—and this to a greater extent as you see the Day drawing nearer. (10:24–25, my translation).

I have to offer my own translation of these verses because many translations just don't get what the author is urging. The NRSV, for example, renders the first of these verses: "let us consider how to provoke one another to love and good deeds." The initial verb, however, calls for observing, noticing, giving careful consideration. And there is nothing in the Greek that suggests any "how to," as if the point of considering the other person is to strategize about how to motivate the other person to do something good for someone else. Rather the object of our observation is to be "one another." We are to take the time and give the attention to one another's circumstances and struggles required so that compassionate love wells up within our own hearts and we ourselves discover how we might serve the other to help him or her bear the burdens and meet the challenges that lie upon and before him or her.

This is a point at which it may be helpful to remember that early Christian congregations regularly met in groups of perhaps twenty to thirty if the congregation had a fairly well-to-do member with a house that could accommodate them, in smaller groups of perhaps ten to fifteen if their host was a well-established artisan or merchant. It is easier to give one another this level of attentiveness in a smaller group than in a congregation of one hundred or more! This is perhaps one reason that small-group ministries have proven so effective in revitalizing churches in the current scene. They allow a smaller circle of Christians to become sufficiently involved and aware of the goings-on in one another's lives that they know when and in what ways assistance would be needed. Indeed, the decision to participate in such small-group ministries ought to be approached not on the basis of what a small group would do for *me*, but on the basis of what involvement in a small group would allow me to do for *others* in the household of God. I have also witnessed how this kind of love-in-action can occur in adult Sunday school classes—particularly those with a core of people who have lived life together for decades—and even church choirs.

It may be that a good number of Christians in North America and Western Europe, especially, need to throw off another set of culturally forged chains; namely, the bondage of thinking we need to project an image of self-sufficiency or self-reliance. The conviction that I can or ought to look after myself and take care of my own problems, and that I would appear weak if I asked for help, is often a symptom of being enslaved to pride. It also becomes a stumbling block to allowing one's sisters and brothers to fulfill their own calling in regard to loving and serving me and, with that, an impediment to allowing the bonds between believers to become as strong as God would wish. We need to allow ourselves to be helped by our sisters and brothers when we find ourselves in some difficulty, because in the harmonious working of God's economy we will always be given an opportunity to offer help to a sister or brother when we have been brought through our own difficulties.

• Questions for Reflection, Discussion, and Action •

What spaces do we make in our lives to learn about the specific needs or challenges that our sisters and brothers face, so that we can discover ways in which we can lay down our time, energies, and/or resources in service to them?

Where does putting yourself at God's disposal to be of assistance, support, or encouragement to other Christians fall in your hierarchy of priorities? If it does not rank where you believe God would have it rank, what changes would you consider making in your life and schedule so as to make yourself more available for God's use for the benefit of your sisters and brothers?

In what ways do you make room for connecting with and serving the needs of sisters and brothers in situations more remote from you, but whose great need cries out nevertheless for you to lay down something of your life for them as well? If God would lead you to make more room, what steps would you take to move in that direction?

• • •

A pervasive theme in the New Testament letters is that God has given each one of us to be a gift to our sisters and brothers in the faith. This theme intersects with the teaching that we are not owners of what is ours—our skills, our abilities, our resources—but, rather, are stewards. God has entrusted all these things to each of us, and done so specifically with a view to our using them in service to one another throughout the household of God:

> Like good stewards of the manifold grace of God, serve one another with whatever gift each of you has received. Whoever speaks must do so as one speaking the very words of God; whoever serves must do so with the strength that God supplies, so that God may be glorified in all things through Jesus Christ. (1 Peter 4:10–11)

Paul approaches the same point from the frame of thinking about the community of faith as a complex, living organism—a body, in which many individual parts make particular contributions to the healthy functioning of the whole:

> For as in one body we have many members, and not all the members have the same function, so we, who are many, are one body in Christ, and individually we are members one of another. We have gifts that differ according to the grace given to us: prophecy, in proportion to faith; ministry, in ministering; the teacher, in teaching; the exhorter, in exhortation; the giver, in generosity; the leader, in diligence; the compassionate, in cheerfulness. (Rom. 12:4–8)

A congregation is an assembly of individuals each of whom has received something from God to offer in service to the others in the community. Paul offers several lists of such gifts (1 Cor. 12:7–11, 28; Eph. 4:11–16), though no single list pretends to be comprehensive. Rather, like the passage from 1 Peter, these offer only examples of the kinds of areas of service in which to offer oneself.

Such texts challenge the common approach that many take to assessing the life of a particular Christian assembly, whether the quality of its worship on the Lord's Day, small groups, adult classes, youth fellowship, children's programs, music programs, or outreach opportunities. The common approach, shaped by the consumer mentality nurtured by our culture, is for an individual to ask: "What did I get out of it?" and evaluate the experience—and even decide whether or not to continue in fellowship with a partic- ular congregation—on that basis. The writers of the New Testament would orient us, rather, to ask: "What has God's Spirit given to me to contribute to the life of this assembly, to build up my sisters and brothers in the faith and to help them carry their burdens? How can I offer myself in service to the household of God in *this* place?"

• Questions for Reflection, Discussion, and Action •

What is the difference between thinking of yourself as the master of your time and resources and thinking of yourself as the steward of the time and resources God has given you in trust? How would those who observe your life place you on the spectrum between master and steward?

What skills, resources, and energies do you currently devote to the life of your local congregation and to the lives of smaller circles of, or even individual, believers? How, in other words, are you contributing to the good of others in the body of Christ?

If there are ways in which God would wish to see you serve other believers, or contribute to the functioning of the body, beyond these, what might they be and what steps might you take to serve God's purposes more fully?

Closing Prayer for Session Five

Lord Jesus, you laid aside the rights and privileges that were yours as the Son of God to serve the Father's purposes for us. You took up a towel to show us that no service is beneath us; when you took up a cross to redeem us, you showed us that no sacrifice is beneath us. Help us grow in our faith so we will trust that the way of serving one another is indeed the way to life and honor in your kingdom. Help us to lay down our own lives in service to your purposes for our sisters and brothers and for those who do not yet know your redemption, until we truly live no more for ourselves, but for you, who died and was raised on our behalf. In your name we pray. Amen.

6

Encourage One Another

Opening Prayer for Session Six

Give us open ears, O Lord, to hear you speaking to us through your Holy Scriptures and through your holy people, our sisters and brothers. Let us clearly discern what your Holy Spirit would say to us this day and let us be sure to obey so that, in our lives and in our life together, we may ever more fully reflect your good and holy desires for us. We ask this in the name of Jesus, our Lord and Redeemer. Amen.

Most New Testament voices are actively involved in encouraging their audiences to take up or to persevere in allegiance to Jesus and the Spirit-led life. Paul, Peter, and the anonymous author of the Letter to the Hebrews, however, also lay upon Christian believers the responsibility of similarly encouraging one another in their ongoing interactions. One online dictionary defines *encouragement* as "the action of giving someone support, confidence, or hope; persuasion to do or to continue something; the act of trying to stimulate the development of an activity, state, or belief."[1] The overlap with the Greek verb used by these New Testament authors is not perfect, but it is significant. It does refer to interactions, often verbal, that have as their goal helping the other person remain committed to a particular course of action or otherwise to sustain them in the face of some challenge. Encouragement takes many forms across the New Testament, and a survey of these forms will expand our own repertoire when it comes to fulfilling our responsibility to help one another maintain our forward momentum toward God's goal for each and all of us.

Honoring someone was a principal means of communicating encouragement in the first-century Roman world. Honor was the recognition—and generally the public recognition—of a person's value to the community. An individual would generally demonstrate this value by having embodied some widely embraced virtue like generosity,

---

1. https://www.lexico.com/definition/encouragement.

piety, or courage. Acknowledging this publicly gave strong inducement to individuals to continue investing themselves in actions that the group valued. Paul himself gives recognition to several Christians by name, encouraging these particular individuals in their efforts and perhaps arousing greater zeal among the audience to rise more fully to the occasions for service that presented themselves:

> I rejoice at the coming of Stephanas and Fortunatus and Achaicus, because they have made up for your absence; for they refreshed my spirit as well as yours. So give recognition to such persons. (1 Cor. 16:17–18)

We should bear in mind that travel in the first century was neither inexpensive nor convenient. Stephanas and his companions put themselves out significantly to travel from Corinth to Ephesus to visit Paul, perhaps bearing the list of issues from the Corinthian congregations on which they sought Paul's guidance (1 Cor. 7:1; 8:1; 12:1; 16:1) and now returning to Corinth with Paul's instructions in written form (1 Corinthians itself!). If Fortunatus and Achaicus were Christian slaves of Stephanas (these are typical slave names), then Stephanas is likely one of the householders providing space and support for a local congregation; he may even have paid for the materials and the scribe who likely produced the final copy of 1 Corinthians. So Paul gives them a bit of special recognition as he closes his letter to the

Corinthian Christians, sending them back with honor. And as they have done the congregations a significant service, he bids these Christian communities also "give recognition to such persons." If a person is traveling in a good direction, a pat on the back can give just enough extra momentum to overcome some weariness or friction in regard to the forward journey.

Paul gives even more lavish recognition in his letter to his friends in Philippi to Timothy for his passion for the gospel and for his selfless service (Phil. 2:19–24) as well as for the service that a certain Philippian Christian named Epaphroditus performed on behalf of both Paul and the local congregation(s) in Philippi (2:25–30). Epaphroditus had traveled from Philippi to visit Paul in prison (perhaps as far away as Rome!), bringing a gift from Paul's friends in Philippi to help support him during his imprisonment. Prisoners generally relied on support from outside for their food and any changes of clothing, not to mention emotional and relational support. If this occurred during Paul's house arrest in Rome, Paul would have been responsible to pay his own rent! In any event, the trip had not been good for Epaphroditus, who fell seriously ill on the journey. He had been recovering, but Paul needed to send him home (again, bearing one of Paul's very precious letters). He honored Epaphroditus, calling him "my brother and co-worker and fellow soldier, your messenger and minister to my need" (Phil. 2:25). He urged the Philippian Christians to "Welcome him then in the Lord with all joy, and honor such people, because he came close to death for the work of Christ, risking his life to make up for those services that you could not give me" (Phil. 2:29–30). Even though the congregation had sent a gift through Epaphroditus, his personal investment in making the trip set him apart—and Paul wanted the believers back home to reward him with honor for that.

When Paul urged the Christians in Rome, then, to "outdo one another in showing honor" (Rom. 12:10), he is urging them to go out of their way to give one another the kind of encouragement that would help each member keep up the momentum of making progress in living a Christ-shaped and other-centered life. Such an instruction was at one and the same time culturally appropriate and highly counter-cultural. Though a person in the first-century Roman world would have shown appropriate honor to those to whom it was due, a person's goal would generally have been to outdo others in receiving honor or being honored rather than in showing honor. This is another example of how Christians have always been called to look out not for their own inter-ests, but for the interests of others (Phil. 2:3). It is in the other person's interest that he or she should receive honor, so I will commit myself to showing him or her honor and, if I distin-guish myself at all, it will not be as the one who is honored, but as the one who honors others.

While we can speak about honor as a core value in the first-century Roman world, it is still a value in the twenty-first century—though we might just call it "being appreciated." Nevertheless, it is every bit as important to affirm godly service as it is to caution against ungodly practices. If you yourself have been told how much your contributions to some enterprise are appreciated or how much your talents are valued, you know the power of the positive reinforcement that such recognition or appreciation brings. Paul wants to see Christian communities full of people who, by means of such affirmation, spur one another on to consistent, ongoing investment in their own progress toward Christlikeness, in the lives of their sisters and brothers, and in the kingdom mission of the global church. Even in the twenty-first century, we need to fight a natural, though unredeemed, tendency to crave honor and recognition for our own service and to feel envy when another is honored, begrudging him or her the same recognition. This calls once again for a shift away from a culture of competition to a culture of cooperation, in which we can genuinely celebrate how each of our sisters and brothers is contributing to the cause of God in their lives, in the community of faith, and in the world.

Paul recognized that a person's contributions were not always obvious—as, indeed, the very capacity to contribute might vary widely from person to person. God has distributed gifts among the members of God's household to use for one another's good, but God has not necessarily distributed them evenly. This, however, cannot be allowed to become the basis for some hierarchy of honor within the congregation. That is how the society around the early Christian communities operated. Paul was clear, however, that it was not to be that way among Christians. Comparing a group of people once more to a single body, he writes:

> On the contrary, the members of the body that seem to be weaker are indispensable, and those members of the body that we think less honorable we clothe with greater honor, and our less respectable members are treated with greater respect; which our more presentable parts do not require. God has so arranged the body, giving the greater honor to the inferior member, that there may be no dissension within the body, but the members may have the same care for one another. (1 Cor. 12:22–25)

Part of the task of encouragement is for us to discover and affirm the value in one another, to help those whose gifts are perhaps less obvious to discover those gifts that God has bestowed upon them for the building up of the whole. Paul's contemporaries treated honor like currency—if I got more, it is only because you came by less. In the household of faith, however, there is more than enough honor to spread it around lavishly.

• Questions for Reflection, Discussion, and Action •

When have you received recognition, small or great, for investing yourself in some act of service in your congregation or other context? How did it make you feel? How did it affect your motivation and/or your sense of connection to the group?

When have you given someone recognition for making a positive impact in some way in your own life or in the life of your congregation? What impact did that have on the other person and on your relationship, to the extent that you can tell?

Who merits recognition in your congregation or other Christian circles right now, and why? What can you do (and will you do) to show that you honor these people?

What sisters and brothers tend to remain invisible when it comes to receiving recognition? What can you do (and will you do) to reinforce for these believers how valued they are and, if appropriate, help them find venues for greater involvement in service?

• • •

We are also called to encourage one another by reminding one another of the foundational truths of God's intervention in the world and in our lives and by keeping one another focused on the fundamentally Godward orientation our lives and our life together are to have. Moving through any given day in their cities, first-century Christians were bombarded with messages—in architecture, in inscriptions, in images on coins, in religious processions and activities, in the speech of their neighbors. These messages promoted another narrative (the gospel of Rome's beneficent rule), other values, and other practices that were incompatible with their new life in Christ. Each of these messages potentially offered the Christian a subtle nudge or, in some cases, a forceful push back toward a life lived in conformity with their society, in alignment with its cherished values, and in pursuit of what it considered good. Early Christian leaders understood the importance of reinforcing for one another the reliability of the new narrative in which they were living. This was the narrative of God's redemption of a people for God's special possession from every nation, tribe, and language group on the earth, for a special destiny that would be realized in the kingdom of his Son. They understood the importance of reinforcing for one another the new values by which they were to live, by which they would live pleasingly in the sight of God, and the higher good after which they were striving together. Thus Paul would advise:

> Be filled with the Spirit, as you sing psalms and hymns and spiritual songs among yourselves, singing and making melody to the Lord in your hearts, giving thanks to God the Father at all times and for everything in the name of our Lord Jesus Christ. (Eph. 5:18–20)

> Let the word of Christ dwell in you richly; teach and admonish one another in all wisdom; and with gratitude in your hearts sing psalms, hymns, and spiritual songs to God. (Col. 3:16)

Singing hymns together, reminding one another of timely Scripture texts, just turning our conversation in the direction of what God has done, is doing, and can do in the midst of our circumstances—all of these things have the power to encourage a sister or brother to remain more firmly oriented toward God, more confident in investing in a Godward life, more hopeful concerning the outcome of a life lived for God.

It is particularly important that we encourage one another—and do so appropriately—at junctures of deep emotional pain and questioning. We each must know that God, our hope in God, and the family of God will not fail us in the face of difficult experiences. Paul knew that the loss of loved ones was such a time, and he wrote specifically to encourage his friends in Thessalonica that their faith and their hope was bigger than death:

> But we do not want you to be uninformed, brothers and sisters, about those who have died, so that you may not grieve as others do who have no hope. For since we believe that Jesus died and rose again, even so, through Jesus, God will bring with him those who have died. . . . For the Lord himself, with a cry of command, with the archangel's call and with the sound of God's trumpet, will descend from heaven, and the dead in Christ will rise first. Then we who are alive, who are left, will be caught up in the clouds together with them to meet the Lord in the air; and so we will be with the Lord forever. Therefore encourage one another with these words. (1 Thess. 4:13–14, 16–18)

The last words are particularly important. Paul charges the believers to keep their shared hope (and, indeed, the firm ground for their hope—here, the resurrection of Jesus himself) before each believer's eyes in the face of grief, a universal human experience that frequently invades the lives of any local congregation. Note the absence of wince-inducing platitudes here. Paul does not say that "God needed another angel" or "God never gives us more than we can handle." He does, however, bid us, as we stand beside a grave, assure our grieving brothers and sisters that Jesus died and rose again specifically to sustain us precisely there, showing us that the grave is not the end.

In the same letter, Paul urges Christ-followers to "encourage one another" in yet another way:

> But since we belong to the day, let us be sober, and put on the breastplate of faith and love, and for a helmet the hope of salvation. For God has destined us not for wrath but for obtaining salvation through our Lord Jesus Christ, who died for us, so that whether we are awake or asleep we may live with him. Therefore encourage one another and build up each other, as indeed you are doing. (1 Thess. 5:8–11)

These words fall at the close of a paragraph that contrasts the messages that people outside of the church were telling one another, resulting in their cluelessness concerning what God was doing in their midst and was yet to do, with the message of our future redemption in the day of the Lord. It was important for Christ-followers to encourage one another in light of that coming day so that each would continue to prioritize living in the present in the way that would prove wisest and most advantageous on *that* day (see also Heb. 10:25). Without that social reinforcement, it is far too easy for us to slip back into living in the way that might give us the greatest advantage and reward now but leave us poor and ashamed on the day of Christ's appearing.

• Questions for Reflection, Discussion, and Action •

What are some of the narratives, values, and pursuits that are out there prominently in your environment that compete for your attention and participation with the grand narrative of God's redemption and the values and pursuits promoted by the Scriptures? When have you found yourself carried away by these to places (whether attitudes, words spoken or written, actions taken) that were in conflict with your formation in Christ?

When has a Christian brother or sister shared a timely word reminding you of God's calling, provision, or expectations that helped you stay centered or regain centeredness in Christ's love and/or the Spirit's leading?

What changes do you need to make in your daily routine and practices to make more room for hearing, celebrating, and sharing the truths of God and his kingdom's priorities, so as to be driven yourself and to help others be driven by these more fully than by the world's alternatives?

• • •

Early Christian leaders relied on Christians' encouragement of one another—their affirmation of one another's honor and value as God's children—to offset the discouragement and resistance that they were experiencing from their non-believing family and neighbors. This was a major issue facing early Christians. In an honor culture such as the first-century Roman world, withholding honor or imposing outright shame was a powerful tool by which to seek to enforce social conformity and to remediate those who had begun to deviate from the larger group's values and practices in significant ways. Reminding one another of the greater honor that they have come to enjoy in the sight of God—and making this real among them in the way that they valued and treasured one another—was much-needed insulation from the corrosive power that shame might exercise over their commitment to Christ and their new family.

This remains a gift we can offer to our sisters and brothers in hostile environments. Many of these Christ-followers have themselves been raised and live in honor cultures and, therefore, are subjected to being shamed by their families, neighbors, and authorities as a means of trying to erode their faith commitment. It can be a great encouragement to them if we, as we learn about their contests, let them know how much we respect and esteem them for their courage and perseverance, even how much their own faith inspires us to exercise greater fortitude in the midst of our far less dramatic and costly challenges.

Sometimes encouragement has to mean more than words spoken from a place of safety as we are called to stand beside—sometimes quite literally—our sisters and brothers who have been particularly targeted by people and powers hostile to the faith and to the directions in which obedience to Christ moves the faithful. Paul and his team were familiar with this need. On one occasion, when it was impossible for Paul himself to return to reassure his friends in Thessalonica, he wrote:

> We sent Timothy, our brother and co-worker for God in proclaiming the gospel of Christ, to strengthen and encourage you for the sake of your faith, so that no one would be shaken by these persecutions. Indeed, you yourselves know that this is what we are destined for. (1 Thess. 3:2–3)

Members of the Christian community or communities to which the Letter to the Hebrews was written had also exhibited the level of commitment to one another that moved those who had not been targeted by their neighbors to publicly identify with their sisters and brothers who had:

> Recall those earlier days when, after you had been
> enlightened, you endured a hard struggle with suffer-
> ings, sometimes being publicly exposed to abuse and
> persecution, and sometimes being partners with
> those so treated. For you had compassion for those
> who were in prison, and you cheerfully accepted the
> plundering of your possessions, knowing that you
> yourselves possessed something better and more
> lasting. (Heb. 10:32–34)

What an encouragement it must have been to the Christ-followers in prison or singled out for public abuse to see their new sisters and brothers in Christ stepping forward and coming beside them in solidarity to show their love and support, thereby inviting the hostility of their neighbors against themselves as well. Their actions showed those most marginalized for their faith that their family in Christ would never desert them, providing them with a support system and a safety net that helped them to persevere.

We also communicate encouragement through the sharing of resources when a sister or brother is in need. Our faithfulness in sharing resources is an important means through which God answers the prayers of our sisters and brothers facing desperate need and, in turn, is our means of demonstrating God's faithfulness to them. It is important to offer this encouragement both locally (as when we see a brother or sister in need; 1 John 3:16–18) and globally (as when we learn or are informed about a situation of need). A thread woven throughout a number of Paul's letters concerns his collection project for the Christians in Jerusalem and Judea, who had been in a vulnerable economic position for years due to the strenuous suppression of the Jesus movement, to sporadic famines, and to the generally growing unrest and volatility of Judea in the decades leading up to the Jewish revolt against Rome that eventually erupted in AD 66. Paul was concerned that his Gentile converts participate generously in this collection project as a sign to Jewish Christians that they really were part of one great family that God had brought together in Christ. But he also saw the tremendous encouragement that the gift would bring:

> The rendering of this ministry not only supplies the needs of the saints but also overflows with many thanksgivings to God.... while they long for you and pray for you because of the surpassing grace of God that he has given you. (2 Cor. 9:12, 14)

The sharing of resources would be received among Judean Christians as an answer to their prayers (hence the multiplying of thanksgiving to God). It would also engender deep affection on the part of Christians in Judea for those believers who, though Gentile by race, had proven themselves to be sisters and brothers in Christ. The sharing of resources among the Christian family, as a well-functioning natural family would share and redistribute resources if need erupted among some members, makes our family connections a reality, particularly for those experiencing lack, but also for those who conscientiously repurpose their goods to meet the needs of these fellow Christians as their family. Nothing says, "You're part of a larger family that has your back," and nothing promotes perseverance in that family and its shared enterprise, like timely help when we find ourselves in need.

• Questions for Reflection, Discussion, and Action •

Who do you know that, because of the situations they are facing, might benefit from the encouragement of other Christians, and perhaps specifically from hearing that they are held in high esteem among their Christian family? What will you do to provide that for a brother or sister this week?

Who needs a little more than that? Who would perhaps benefit from your physical presence to embolden them as they face some difficulty or seek to overcome some challenge in their situations?

What members of your congregation or other Christian circles would receive significant encouragement through their brothers and sisters coming alongside them with material or other needful, timely assistance? How might God wish to meet their need—and answer their prayer—through you?

Closing Prayer for Session Six

Almighty God, you have bestowed on all who believe in your Son the honor of being adopted as your own sons and daughters. You have set before us the hope of glory and set behind us the examples of generations of your followers who have run the race well. You have given us as gifts to our sisters and brothers in Christ and given them as gifts to us. Help us to keep one another mindful of the esteem in which you hold us, especially when a sister or brother suffers shame for the faith; help us to hold before one another the hope that draws us forward and the witness that impels us forward. Open our eyes to every opportunity to encourage our sisters and brothers to hold onto your gifts and promises, to invest themselves fully in the work of faith and love, and to resist every temptation to draw back from your calling. We ask this in Jesus' name. Amen.

7

Watch Over One Another

Opening Prayer for Session Seven

Give us open ears, O Lord, to hear you speaking to us through your Holy Scriptures and through your holy people, our sisters and brothers. Let us clearly discern what your Holy Spirit would say to us this day and let us be sure to obey so that, in our lives and in our life together, we may ever more fully reflect your good and holy desires for us. We ask this in the name of Jesus, our Lord and Redeemer. Amen.

When God inquired into Abel's whereabouts, Cain famously asked: "Am I my brother's keeper?" (Gen. 4:9). Cain assumed that the answer was self-evidently:

"Of course not." He was wrong—at least, from the perspective of the early Christian leaders who wrote what has become our New Testament. Against the modern, Western trend to regard our faith and practice as something that we are free to work out privately between ourselves and God, these early Christian leaders would challenge us to lower the privacy screens we place between us and our sisters and brothers in Christ, both so that we can watch over them and so they can watch over us.

The members of the house churches addressed by the Letter to the Hebrews had experienced considerable pressure from their non-Christian neighbors to back off from their commitment to this new "cult" (that is, the Christian faith!). They wanted them to take up again the practices that bound them to their non-Christian neighbors and reinforced the values of the larger society, whether close observance of the Jewish law and the proper boundaries between Jews and Gentiles or a return to the social and religious activities of the Gentile population. The Christ-followers had met this pressure head-on in the earlier days of their faith journey (Heb. 10:32–35), but over time the shaming and sidelining were beginning to take their toll—to the point that some of their number had already visibly drawn back from Christian fellowship and from association with this unpopular movement (Heb. 10:25).

The member of Paul's team who wrote the Letter to the Hebrews well understood the value of social reinforcement of a believer's commitment to discipleship within the Christian assemblies for increasing the likelihood of that individual withstanding the social deterrents from without. And so he gives these instructions:

> Take care, brothers and sisters, that none of you may have an evil, unbelieving heart that turns away from the living God. But exhort one another every day, as long as it is called "today," so that none of you may be hardened by the deceitfulness of sin. For we have become partners of Christ, if only we hold our first confidence firm to the end. (Heb. 3:12–14)

It's helpful here if we look a bit behind the New Revised Standard Version (NRSV) at the author's actual words. The opening command is something more like "Watch out," or "Be on the lookout." He also uses a plural form of the command, so his audience would hear something along the lines of "Y'all be on the lookout lest any one among y'all" exhibits these symptoms. In other words, he is very clearly commending the spiritual care of each individual member to all the other members of these assemblies. He gives all of us together the responsibility for facilitating the perseverance of any one among us. Though we face different social pressures in North America than those faced by the congregations addressed by Hebrews, the need to watch over one another and the need to "exhort one another"—to keep one another focused on the priorities and goals that God's work in and through our lives sets before us—remains constant.

In their context, sin's deceitfulness worked through their neighbors' attempts to convince them that Christ's gifts, friendship, and promises were not worth what it was costing to keep them. In our context, sin's deceitfulness may work by convincing us that religion may have its place in a full life, but shouldn't distract us from the important matters of business or politics or take over to the extent that we don't enjoy the lifestyle and entertainments our context affords us. We run less the risk of "turning away from the living God" and more the risk of making the living God into our household god to whom we give the occasional nod so that we might have his blessing as we live our lives. Whatever sin's means of deceiving, we need one another to help us not lose sight of what the living God merits in terms of our priorities and investments.

The author of Hebrews gives similar instructions toward the end of his sermon, once again commending the perseverance of each individual to the watchful care of the group:

> See to it that no one fails to obtain the grace of God;
> that no root of bitterness springs up and causes
> trouble, and through it many become defiled. See

> to it that no one becomes like Esau, an immoral and
> godless person, who sold his birthright for a single
> meal. You know that later, when he wanted to inherit
> the blessing, he was rejected, for he found no chance
> to repent, even though he sought the blessing with
> tears. (Heb. 12:15–17)

Once again it may be helpful to look behind the NRSV. The word rendered "See to it" could be better rendered "Exercise watchful care." It is the word for exercising oversight, for "looking out" for those entrusted to one's care. And once again it is a plural form, charging all the members of the group to "exercise watchful care" over each individual member—to watch over one another.

The way the author expresses what is at stake is also worth attention. "Failing to obtain God's grace" is not the most helpful translation. I would suggest we hear this more along the lines of "falling short of God's gift"—even as the exodus generation, to which the author of Hebrews gave significant attention earlier in his sermon, fell short of entering the promised land because of their lack of trust and commitment to obey (Heb. 3:7–4:11). Alternatively, we might hear it as "not making it all the way that God's favor would take us," again because lack of trust and commitment derailed us along the way or, at the very least, slowed our progress. This is especially relevant to disciples swimming in the Wesleyan streams of the faith, for we believe that God's

favor toward us extends well beyond his forgiveness of sin
as far as God's transforming us into people in whom his
love flows in such fullness that there is no room left for sin.
If we are not to fall short of God's goal for us, however, we
certainly need to "exercise watchful care" over one another,
encouraging, motivating, and holding one another accountable to our own better desires for ourselves.

• Questions for Reflection and Discussion •

Can you recall one or two episodes when a timely word or
conversation with a brother or sister in the Lord helped you
to continue in a direction toward godly goals rather than
lose heart or, perhaps, even turn in a direction that would
not please God?

Can you recall, similarly, one or two episodes when you
intervened healthfully in this way for a brother or sister in
the Lord?

By contrast, can you recall an episode in which, looking
back, you would now have wished that a brother or sister
was watching out for you more closely—or you for a
brother or sister—so as perhaps to have avoided a detour in
a faith journey?

• • •

The watchful care that we are challenged to exercise regarding one another includes, of course, watching over one another in prayer. The New Testament letters frequently urge believers to pray not just for their own needs and concerns, but specifically for the needs and concerns for their sisters and brothers:

> Pray in the Spirit at all times in every prayer and supplication. To that end keep alert and always persevere in supplication for all the saints. Pray also for me . . . (Eph. 6:18–19)

> As for other matters, brothers and sisters, pray for us that the message of the Lord may spread rapidly and be honored, just as it was with you. (2 Thess. 3:1 NIV)

> Brothers and sisters, pray for us. (1 Thess. 5:25 NIV)

> Pray for us, for we are sure that we have a clear conscience, desiring to act honorably in all things. I urge you the more earnestly to do this in order that I may be restored to you the sooner. (Heb. 13:18–19 ESV)

If we are to "persevere in supplication for all the saints," we must open our eyes and ears to their condition. We must hold them in our hearts as we go before our common Lord. This is a spiritual discipline that, on the one hand, changes us by exercising us in being concerned for the interests of others, of being other-centered in our prayers. It trains us to seek the good of our sisters and brothers, first from the Lord in prayer and, as a corollary, through what the Lord might prompt us to do to advance their good.

We believe, on the other hand, that prayer is truly an effective means of connecting our sisters and brothers with the favor of God. Testimonies abound to prayer being effective in ways that we cannot easily understand. A Russian Christian named Alexander Ogorodnikov was imprisoned for eight years for his faith. At one point he was near breaking. His tormentors used the extreme cold temperature to their advantage. It was making Alexander desperate, but he could find no way to escape the cold or get warm. As he himself went to prayer, he reports: "I felt warm breathing, and the lovely touch of a brother's hand. I cried like a child, and understood it was a prayer for me. It helped me to survive."[1] Christians who suffer persecution in countries that also have fairly broad access to the Internet are frequently encouraged as they visit websites that show the

---

1. Barbara von der Heydt, *Candles behind the Wall: Heroes of the Peaceful Revolution That Shattered Communism* (Grand Rapids, MI: Eerdmans, 1993), 39.

prayers posted on their behalf by their sisters and brothers throughout the world.[2] The yearning of the hearts of one's brothers and sisters before God on one's behalf communicates strength to endure in the "long obedience in the same direction" that is Christian discipleship.[3]

There is a temptation, however, to think that prayers ought primarily to be focused upon the urgent needs of our bodies or circumstances, focusing on asking God for help in the midst of sickness, surgery, a period of unemployment, relationship challenges, and the like. The prayers we encounter in the New Testament suggest that, while these are indeed suitable subjects for prayer, our yearnings for one another before God penetrate much deeper. The apostle Paul appears to have been ever in prayer before God on behalf of those who had come to faith through his ministry and that of his team. His prayers were often focused on his sisters' and brothers' progress in living ever more fully the life into which their trust in Jesus had initiated them, making ever fuller use of God's provisions for their growth and transformation, and attaining the fullness of God's goals for them:

---

2. For one such site in the English-speaking world, visit https://www.icommittopray.com/.

3. The quote is from Friedrich Nietzsche, *Beyond Good and Evil*, trans. Walter Kaufmann (New York: Random House, 1966), 99.

And this is my prayer, that your love may overflow
more and more with knowledge and full insight to
help you to determine what is best, so that in the
day of Christ you may be pure and blameless, having
produced the harvest of righteousness that comes
through Jesus Christ for the glory and praise of God.
(Phil. 1:9–11)

We have not ceased praying for you and asking that
you may be filled with the knowledge of God's will
in all spiritual wisdom and understanding, so that
you may lead lives worthy of the Lord, fully pleasing
to him, as you bear fruit in every good work and as
you grow in the knowledge of God. (Col. 1:9–10)

To this end we always pray for you, asking that our
God will make you worthy of his call and will fulfill
by his power every good resolve and work of faith,
so that the name of our Lord Jesus may be glorified
in you, and you in him, according to the grace of our
God and the Lord Jesus Christ. (2 Thess. 1:11–12)

Paul's prayers on behalf of his converts are very infor-
mative for the kinds of supplications we might consider
bringing into our prayers on our own behalf and on behalf
of our sisters and brothers. I can readily imagine the impact
that hearing Paul's reports of his prayers would have had
on his audiences. It would have potentially reinforced

their own desires to see these same things accomplished in their own lives and those of their fellow disciples. It would have called their attention afresh to these things as pursuits and goals to prioritize among themselves, seeking God's provision—in unison with their brother Paul—for making progress in these holy directions. How much more, then, would it have helped each member of these house assemblies if, in their prayers together, these petitions lived on as constant reminders of what they ought to be desiring and seeking from God for themselves and for one another, informing the ways in which they would also watch over one another in their day-to-day and week-to-week interactions?

John adds yet another dimension to our watching over one another in prayer. This one might strike us as somewhat strange, for it has to do with asking God to forgive not ourselves, but our sister or brother whom we see committing some sin:

> And this is the boldness we have in him, that if we ask anything according to his will, he hears us. And if we know that he hears us in whatever we ask, we know that we have obtained the requests made of him. If you see your brother or sister committing what is not a mortal sin, you will ask, and God will give life to such a one—to those whose sin is not mortal. (1 John 5:14–16)

The first few sentences remind us of the great assurance that Jesus has given us; namely, that God will hear and grant the prayers we offer. But John reminds us of this privilege specifically to recommend that we pray forgiveness over our sisters and brothers when they commit some sin. The NRSV may not be doing us a favor when it renders "a sin leading to death" as "a mortal sin." The latter phrase carries the baggage of the Roman Catholic church's historic division of sins into the categories of "venial" and "mortal" and the requirement of confession and penance if one is to obtain absolution for "mortal" sins. John more likely reflects here a more vivid awareness that there are simply some affronts against God that lead to a person dropping dead. It happened to Ananias and Sapphira (Acts 5:1–11). It appears to have happened to some members of one or more house churches in Corinth, though even there Paul affirmed the possibility of self-examination, confession, and restoration (1 Cor. 11:27–32). Such testimonies to the incompatibility of sin in the community of faith with the holiness of the God who dwells in our midst should motivate us to take sin with the utmost seriousness when it erupts in our own lives or in the lives of our sisters and brothers.

It might be tempting to distract ourselves by trying to answer the impossible question of "How do you know when someone has committed a 'sin unto death' for which we are not necessarily to pray?" I would rather that we focus on the extraordinary instruction here that we pray on another's behalf that God would forgive that person at all. This represents a very different kind of response to seeing a brother or sister moving in a harmful direction than, say, gossiping or complaining to others about their words or actions. John suggests that our intercession on behalf of one another in regard to the sins that don't make us drop dead is effective before God. Such a practice, moreover, would certainly change our own hearts and inclinations toward one another when we see those among us moving in directions in which the pursuit of God's favor would not take them.

• Questions for Reflection, Discussion, and Action •

How much attention do you give in prayer to the challenges and areas of need facing your Christian brothers and sisters near and far? How might you regularly make more space for such supplication in your life, if more would be appropriate?

To what extent do your prayers mirror the kinds of prayer Paul offered for his brothers and sisters in the Lord? How might it change your own focus and priorities if you were to give more room to praying for your own and fellow believers' growth and transformation?

How would it change the culture of your congregation if people prayed for those whom they believe to have sinned rather than gossip or complain about their actions?

Using Paul's prayers (you might also look at Ephesians 1:17–19; 3:14–21), spend some time in prayer for yourself and for three of your fellow disciples. If at all possible, pray these things together with them.

• • •

Meeting regularly in small groups provides obvious advantages for fulfilling the scriptural charge to watch over one another. As we grow in our knowledge of one another, we also increase our ability to discern the signs that a sister or brother needs our encouragement to persevere in the direction of attaining all that God, in God's grace, desires for her or him to attain. Instituting such regular meetings among Christians lay at the heart of John Wesley's renewal movement. He described these small groups, which he called "classes" (groups of about ten to twelve), as "a company of men [and women] having the form and seeking the power of godliness, united in order to pray together, to receive the word of exhortation, and to watch over one another in love, that they may help each other to work out their salvation."[4] The agenda of these groups was simple—to check in with one another and to inquire of each whether he or she was "growing closer to Christ or falling further away."[5] Sharing this information with a small group opened up the door to the kinds of encouragement of one another and the kinds of prayer with one another that allowed each member to receive God's grace to persevere. This required a commitment to transparency on the part of each member as well as a commitment to meet the transparency of the other members with a gentleness that proved worthy of such trust, holding one another's spiritual condition lovingly before the Father.

The rewards of stepping forward together in such mutual trust, moreover, were significant. In his "Plain Account of the People Called Methodists," Wesley says of these meetings:

> Advice or reproof was given as needed, quarrels made up, misunderstandings removed. And after an hour or two spent in this labour of love, they concluded with prayer and thanksgiving. . . . Many now happily

---

4. John Wesley, "The Nature, Design, and General Rules of the United Societies," in *The Works of John Wesley*, Bicentennial Edition (Nashville, TN: Abingdon, 1989), 9:69.

5. Kevin Watson, *The Class Meeting: Reclaiming a Forgotten (and Essential) Small Group Experience* (Franklin, TN: Seedbed Publishing, 2014), 28.

experienced that Christian fellowship of which they had not so much as an idea before. They began to "bear one another's burdens," and naturally to "care for each another." As they had daily a more intimate acquaintance with, so they had a more endeared affection for, each other.[6]

Wesley understood what the early Christian leaders knew so well: we need one another if we are to arrive at the fullness of the personal transformation the Holy Spirit seeks to work within us and experience the depth of fellowship, support, and love that God intends to characterize the family that he has brought together in Christ. The more isolationist form of discipleship rarely produces growth and all too often leaves room for "the deceitfulness of sin" (Heb. 3:13) to stall—if not make shipwreck of—our faith journey.

• Questions for Reflection, Discussion, and Action •

Have you had the experience of meeting in a small group where you felt that you were genuinely "watching over one another in love"? How did that experience sustain and

---

6. John Wesley, "A Plain Account of the People Called Methodists," in *Works*, 9:262.

nurture your faith and transformation? If there was a down-side to the experience, what was that?

How would you feel about being a part of a group such as Wesley's first Methodists committed to? How might it nurture the quality of connection and interpersonal inter-actions that we have been exploring throughout our study? What reservations might you have about belonging to such a group?

If you decide that belonging to such a group would both give you support and allow you to lend support to others in their faith journey, what steps are available to you to finding or starting such a group?

Closing Prayer for Session Seven

Lord Jesus, we thank you for the family that you have given us, that you have entrusted to our care, and to whose care you have entrusted us. Help us to watch over one another in love more and more effectively. Lead us to take the time and make the opportunities to check in with one another and to discover if a sister or brother is in need of some particular help or intervention. Give us the wisdom we need to offer timely counsel, support, and assistance in a manner that can most readily be received. Give us also the humility to accept the same from our sisters and brothers when we stand in need of their care. We ask this in your name. Amen.

8

Restore One Another

Opening Prayer for Session Eight

Give us open ears, O Lord, to hear you speaking to us through your Holy Scriptures and through your holy people, our sisters and brothers. Let us clearly discern what your Holy Spirit would say to us this day and let us be sure to obey so that, in our lives and in our life together, we may ever more fully reflect your good and holy desires for us. We ask this in the name of Jesus, our Lord and Redeemer. Amen.

We've looked at Jesus' instructions concerning two people dealing with the offense that has come between them and interrupted the harmony of God's family.

Here we turn to a related, but larger, more uncomfortable, and more difficult aspect of our responsibility to one another in Christ; namely, our responsibility to intervene when a brother or sister has strayed from living in line with the holiness and righteousness to which we are called and for which we have been redeemed.

I have reserved this facet of the New Testament vision for Christian community for the last chapter of this study because the kinds of interaction envisioned here—and the likelihood of individuals undertaking or accepting the kinds of interventions envisioned here—depend on two critically important things: trust and trustworthiness. Individual believers must be able to trust the goodwill and sincere motivations of others in the group to accept such interventions, and the members who make up the group must have proven themselves trustworthy so as to rightly nurture such trust. Only the members of those Christian communities that have significantly invested themselves in welcoming, encouraging, loving, and serving one another will have the moral authority and interpersonal connections necessary to engage one another at this deeper level.

We encountered Jesus' instructions in Matthew 18:15–20 already in the context of the mandate to forgive, and seek forgiveness from, one another. But there is an important alternative reading in the two earliest Greek manuscripts of this Gospel that have survived, manuscripts that go

back to the fourth century AD. Instead of starting out
with the phrase "If your brother or sister sins against you"
(Matt. 18:15 CEB), these manuscripts read simply: "If your
brother or sister sins." In context, this becomes: "If your
brother or sister sins, go lay bare the matter between the
two of you alone. And if he or she listens to you, you won
back your brother or sister" (Matt. 18:15, my translation).
Jesus himself is elsewhere remembered to have instructed
his followers to "Be on your guard! If another disciple sins,
you must rebuke the offender, and if there is repentance,
you must forgive" (Luke 17:3), a rather close parallel to this
variant reading.

This extends the applicability of Jesus' mandate—and
our responsibility—considerably. I am charged not just with
dealing in a healthy manner with the toxins that a brother
or sister's offense against me has introduced into my relationship with him or her, but also with dealing with the
toxins that a brother or sister's offense against God or against
anyone has introduced into his or her relationships with God
and with the family of God's people. In these manuscripts,
then, I am charged to take even greater risk by speaking with
a brother or sister about something I observed in his or her
behavior rather than remain silent beyond those things that
have impacted me personally.

If the conversation results in my brother or sister
acknowledging the problem and moving in a corrective

direction (unless the conversation reveals that I misunderstood what I observed), that would be a win. If not, then the family becomes involved in increasing numbers in a kind of escalating intervention, seeking to bring the brother or sister back to embrace the values or practices that he or she had begun to abandon:

> "But if you are not listened to, take one or two others along with you, so that every word may be confirmed by the evidence of two or three witnesses. If the member refuses to listen to them, tell it to the church; and if the offender refuses to listen even to the church, let such a one be to you as a Gentile and a tax collector. Truly I tell you, whatever you bind on earth will be bound in heaven, and whatever you loose on earth will be loosed in heaven. Again, truly I tell you, if two of you agree on earth about anything you ask, it will be done for you by my Father in heaven. For where two or three are gathered in my name, I am there among them." (Matt. 18:16–20)

The second step in the intervention involves inviting one or more fellow believers into the conversation, not necessarily because they were witnesses to some particular sin, but because they can bear witness that a particular attitude or behavior is indeed sin and, therefore, something from which to repent and seek God's grace to leave behind. They are to confirm that the subject is not just one member's pet peeve, but reflects a value shared by the group. The brother or sister who has been straying has to come to terms here with the fact that his or her choices have not been in alignment with the Spirit-shaped life for which we were redeemed.

If the individual remains unconvinced, the whole assembly (which, we should remember, would have likely numbered no more than twenty or thirty) is brought into the conversation in an attempt to encourage the individual to return to a more sanctified practice. If the individual continues to refuse correction, there is really no more room for him or her in the company of those who are moving together in a different direction. Notice here the context of the oft-quoted passage about two disciples agreeing in prayer or the assurance of Jesus' presence "where two or three are gathered in my name." These statements are made specifically in the context of community discipline—the intervention of some Christians in the life of a straying brother or sister with a view to his or her reclamation. Jesus invests the body of disciples with significant authority to discern together the boundaries of attitude and practice, on the one side of which lies alignment with the group and on the other side of which lies incompatibility with the group. Indeed, he promises to be present specifically in this process of mutual restoration.

We could make another important observation from
the context of Jesus' instructions concerning our intervening healthfully in the life of a brother or sister who has
moved away from walking in Jesus' teaching and example.
In Matthew's Gospel, these instructions are preceded by the
parable of the lost sheep:

> "Take care that you do not despise one of these little
> ones; for, I tell you, in heaven their angels continu-
> ally see the face of my Father in heaven. What do you
> think? If a shepherd has a hundred sheep, and one of
> them has gone astray, does he not leave the ninety-
> nine on the mountains and go in search of the one
> that went astray? And if he finds it, truly I tell you, he
> rejoices over it more than over the ninety-nine that
> never went astray. So it is not the will of your Father
> in heaven that one of these little ones should be lost."
> (Matt. 18:10–14)

In Luke's Gospel, this same parable is used in the context
of a dispute between Jesus and other Jewish religious experts.
There the parable is used to illustrate Jesus' own mission to
seek and to save the lost. Here, however, the parable underscores the importance of keeping those who have previously
been brought into Jesus' fold walking in his paths. The
instructions that follow, then, lay out the community of

disciples' part in helping ensure that "not . . . one of these little ones should be lost."

• Questions for Reflection and Discussion •

Have you had the experience of a brother or sister in Christ taking you aside and helping you identify some area in which you were not walking in line with the Spirit? What was the outcome of that experience, both in your own life and in your relationship with that fellow disciple?

Have you taken that same initiative with a brother or sister in Christ? Again, what were the outcomes?

Can you recall one or more times when, in hindsight, you might wish to have taken that initiative—or that someone had taken that initiative with you?

• • •

Passages from the New Testament letters also speak about our responsibility to restore one another to the path of holiness and love when we see one another moving in directions contrary to "a manner that is worthy of the calling to which [we] have been called" (Eph. 4:1). Indeed, they are so numerous it is surprising to find such interventions in one another's lives so rarely practiced in the church. Paul, for example, gives clear expression to this dimension of our obligation to one another in the community of faith:

> My friends, if anyone is detected in a transgression, you who have received the Spirit should restore such a one in a spirit of gentleness. Take care that you yourselves are not tempted. Bear one another's burdens, and in this way you will fulfill the law of Christ. (Gal. 6:1–2)

Paul has spent the greater part of Galatians demonstrating that, on this side of the coming of Christ, God intends for God's people to follow and be formed by the Holy Spirit rather than the law of Moses. He has assured his converts that the Spirit-formed life would accomplish all that the Law had ever sought to achieve in terms of shaping human behavior and interaction. But Paul also knows that we will not always fully "keep in step with the Spirit" (Gal. 5:25 NIV) but run the risk of being misled by our own self-serving inclinations and desires—by "the deceitfulness of sin" (to borrow a phrase from Hebrews 3:13). For just such eventualities, God has supplied each of us with the necessary guardrails to get us back on track—our brothers and sisters in Christ! Our discernment together of what impulses and actions originate from the Spirit rather than from our self-centeredness, and our willingness to keep one another on track in regard to the former, constitute the safety net for living in freedom from the written code of the Law.

Paul instructs us, when coming alongside an errant sister or brother, to suggest a course correction, to do so in a spirit of "gentleness"—not incidentally a manifestation of the Spirit's fruit in our own lives (Gal. 5:23). We are not given license to use another's stepping into sin as an opportunity to puff ourselves up or bring shame upon the other, but are charged with approaching him or her with the humility and sympathy that come from knowing our own vulnerability to temptation and from realizing how we ourselves have needed and will need again such intervention in our lives on our sisters' or brothers' part. Helping one another recognize where sin is gaining a foothold again in our lives, and praying with and strengthening one another against those incursions, is one way in which we "bear one another's burdens, and so fulfill the law of Christ" (Gal. 6:2 ESV). It is a practical expression of loving my neighbor as myself, since I take up my neighbor's burden alongside him or her as my own and commit to his or her restoration.

James and Jude speak in unison with Jesus and Paul on this point, urging believers to invest themselves in helping one another to recognize when they are veering off the Spirit's course and to find their way back:

> My brothers and sisters, if anyone among you wanders from the truth and is brought back by another, you should know that whoever brings back a sinner from wandering will save the sinner's soul from death and will cover a multitude of sins. (James 5:19–20)

> But you, beloved, build yourselves up on your most holy faith; pray in the Holy Spirit; keep yourselves in the love of God; look forward to the mercy of our Lord Jesus Christ that leads to eternal life. And have mercy on some who are wavering; save others by snatching them out of the fire; and have mercy on still others with fear, hating even the tunic defiled by their bodies. (Jude 20–23)

Fulfilling these mandates requires of us that we engage in the uncomfortable—and, in the current climate, unpopular—activity of discernment, making a judgment call that some behavior that we're observing doesn't line up with God's best wishes for his people. This should be done with humility, more in the mode of inquiry than indictment, if only to be sure that we are dealing gently with our sister or brother, and also with a single-hearted commitment to seek God's best for our sister or brother. Whatever Jesus meant when he enjoined his hearers, "Do not judge, so that you may not be judged" (Matt. 7:1), he clearly did not intend to exclude us from engaging in these processes of restoring one another, for which he and his apostles gave far more extensive and explicit instructions.

While we might find these instructions difficult to put into practice, the alternative to confronting and restoring is often far less kind. You may have witnessed this alternative in your own congregational experience; I know that I have. A husband married for more than thirty years decides that his marriage is unsatisfying and begins an affair with a much younger woman. No one confronts him about his choices or calls it sin. Rather, they quietly condemn his actions (though not quietly among themselves when he's not in the room, of course). They grow cold toward him and treat him differently enough that eventually he leaves the fellowship unchallenged and unrestored to the life of holiness and self-giving for which Christ had redeemed him. Paul instructed his congregations to take such a person aside, identify the sinful outcome of a series of choices, and pray with him or her for his or her restoration: "Don't regard him [or her] as an enemy, but warn him [or her] as a brother [or sister]" (2 Thess. 3:15 ESV). Too often, because of an aversion to initiating difficult conversations and interventions, we find it easier to pull back and treat the wayward brother or sister as an enemy, even if only in passive-aggressive ways.

• Questions for Reflection and Discussion •

Can you recall one or two incidents where a member or two of a congregation of which you were (or are) a part began to live in a way clearly outside of the instructions of Jesus and the New Testament writers? How did other members of the congregation respond? What was the outcome in the faith journey of the errant member or members?

What are the pros and cons of belonging to a congregation or small group where members invest themselves in keeping one another on track with their own best intentions for themselves? Is this a dimension you would wish to experience and promote in your Christian circles?

• • •

Toward the end of his collection of wise instruction for living together as communities of disciples, James wrote:

> Are any among you sick? They should call for the
> elders of the church and have them pray over them,
> anointing them with oil in the name of the Lord. The
> prayer of faith will save the sick, and the Lord will
> raise them up; and anyone who has committed sins
> will be forgiven. Therefore confess your sins to one
> another, and pray for one another, so that you may be
> healed. (James 5:14–16)

The culture of the early Methodist movement was purposefully and explicitly a culture of watching over and restoring one another in love. Wesley organized these Methodists in small bands, which were even smaller groups than his classes (perhaps only four or five people). Concerning these bands, Wesley wrote: "The design of our meeting is to obey that command of God, 'Confess your faults one to another, and pray one for another, that ye may be healed.'" The agenda for these bands was simple. Their members would gather "once a week, at the least, . . . to speak each of us in order, freely and plainly, the true state of our souls, with the faults we have committed in thought, word, or deed, and the temptations we have felt, since our last meeting," and then "to end every meeting with prayer, suited to the state of each person present."[1] Before a person

---

1. Wesley's "Rules for Band-Societies," drawn up December 25, 1738.

was admitted as a member of a band society, he or she had to agree to speak openly and honestly and give others permission to freely voice their concerns about his or her walk before the Lord.

It might seem terribly daunting to step into such a group, though it is helpful to remember that such groups tend to emerge in the contemporary scene more organically from circles of people who have already learned to trust one another in other settings. At the same time, without the intentionality of forming and belonging to such a group, it is difficult to find the level of commitment and intimacy in congregational settings that allows us to form the kinds of mutually supporting relationships that were taken for granted in the early church. Simply put, we need one another's encouragement and intervention if we are to escape being "hardened by the deceitfulness of sin" (Heb. 3:12–13, my translation) and if we are to "make it all the way that God's favor would take us" (Heb. 12:15, my translation). It is my sincerest prayer that every Christ-follower will be intent on experiencing the fullness of the deliverance from sin's power (and not just sin's penalty!) that Jesus has won for us, and that they will find—or form—the bands of disciples that will sustain them all the way to the end of that journey.

• Questions for Reflection,
Discussion, and Action •

When, if ever, have you found strength to deal with temptation or to extract yourself from some sinful practice through confessing the temptation or sin to one or more brothers or sisters in Christ, through praying together over the matter, and through ongoing accountability?

Are there two or three people in your life right now with whom you could do such a thing if and when the need arises? Who would these people be?

Consider an experiment. Invite those two or three others to meet to talk about where each of you finds yourself in your walk with God and where each of you would like to find yourself in that walk. Pray for each other, that God would lead each of you closer to that end. After a few days, check in with one another to see if meeting again might be part of God's leading.

Closing Prayer for Session Eight

Almighty God, you have set all of us who call upon the name of your Son Jesus upon a journey of transformation, and you have charged each of us with helping our sisters and brothers find the strength and support they need to persevere in that journey in the face of the many temptations that we all encounter. Help us to nurture such harmony, love, and trust among our fellowship that we may honestly confess our temptations to one another before they become sins. May we receive strength from one another to resist temptations and to invest ourselves in greater holiness. Grant us also the courage to risk coming alongside a sister or brother who may be falling into temptation and the wisdom to approach in such a way as allows defenses to be lowered and help to be received. Deepen our fellowship, gracious Lord, so that we may fully be for one another the gifts and the community of support that you intended for us to be. We ask all this in the name of Jesus. Amen.

9 781628 249125